EMBLEMS IN SHAKESPEARE'S LAST PLAYS

Kwang Soon Cho

University Press of America, Inc.
Lanham • New York • Oxford

Copyright © 1998 by
University Press of America,® Inc.
4720 Boston Way
Lanham, Maryland 20706

12 Hid's Copse Rd.
Cummor Hill, Oxford OX2 9JJ

Library of Congress Cataloging-in-Publication Data

Cho, Kwang Soon.
Emblems in Shakespear's last plays / Kwang Soon Cho.
p. cm.
Revision of the author's thesis (Ph.D.)—Michigan State University,
1990.
Includes bibliographical references and index.
1. Shakespeare, William, 1564-1616—Tragicomedies. 2.
Emblems—England—History—17th century. 3. Emblems in
literature. 4. Tragicomedy. I. Title.
PR2981.5C47   1997   822.3'3—dc21   97—39862 CIP

ISBN 0-7618-0932-5 (cloth: alk. ppr.)

Laus Deo in Excelsis

CONTENTS

List of Plates

Preface

This study is an essay on the question of how Shakespeare uses emblems in his last plays to address significant moral and ethical themes. It, however, is not a kind of source hunting whose validity has been often called into question. Rather it focuses on the multilayeredness of meanings in emblems which provides us with a fresh and integral perspective on interpreting the plays. When the plays are approached from this frame of reference, they reveal some thematic nexus which remain hitherto unexplored. Through this effort, we fully understand the symbolic aspect of the plays overcoming the naive idea that they should be taken at face value. Especially in the last plays symbolism is more rampant than in any other category of Shakespeare's plays. For this reason, five of the last plays are examined as a group in this study. I direct my attention not only to the question of multifaceted meanings in the last plays, but to that of the different modes of representation in the play and in the poem. To deal with these issues, in the introduction I discuss in detail several important aspects of emblems. I hope that the introduction serves as my ancillary effort to help the reader to more fully recognize the rich and profound world of the emblem which is essential for appreciating Shakespeare's last plays.

It is a pleasure to acknowledge my indebtedness to those who have helped me to shape this study. Of my professors at Michigan State University, I must first give my hearty and warm thanks to Jay Ludwig, whose suggestions and comments have paved the groundwork for this project. Douglas Peterson introduced me to the fascinating literary world of the Renaissance and the emblem. His *Time, Tide, and Tempest*, is one of the books with which I have consulted. I am also as much indebted to Donald Rosenberg, Philip McGuire, and Marcellette Williams who served me as three other readers of my thesis from which this study has developed.

To those listed above, I must add some more names. I give thanks to Professor Sang Deuk Moon for his encouragement and help. I also express my gratitude to Nancy Ulrich and Helen Hudson at University Press of America who have assisted me in coping with many practical problems. My typist, Chasun Kim, has done editing jobs. My wife, Heesook, is a cherub who has preserved me with her smile "infused with a fortitude from heaven" (*The Tempest* I.ii 154).

Last but not least, I express my acknowledgement to the Daewoo Scholarship Foundation in Seoul for the fund which has satisfied the requirements for publication. Ajou University has granted me financial support for the cost of preparing the camera-ready pages. The British Council in Seoul has provided me with a travel grant. Slightly different versions of the chapter on *Pericles* and on *Henry VIII* appeared in *The Journal of English Language and Literature* (39:4 [1993]) and *Shakespeare Review* (No. 30 [1997]) respectively.

CHAPTER 1

Introduction

The purpose of this study is to show how Shakespeare in his last plays uses emblem and emblematic scenes to control audience response. The value of such a study lies in showing how through such scenes he conveys his moral and ethical vision to the audience.

Before demonstrating how the playwright controls the audience with emblem and emblematic scenes, it is necessary to define terminology. By "response" I mean the audience's mental activities during the performance of a play. In this sense response is interchangeable with effect. The term "emblem" refers to a popular form of literature throughout the European Renaissance. According to Peter Daly, more than two thousand emblem books were produced in Europe during the sixteenth and seventeenth centuries.[1] In England six emblem books were published during the sixteenth century.[2] Emblem literature formed an important aspect of Renaissance literature. Emblems proper consist of three parts: motto (*inscriptio*), picture (*pictura*), and poem (*subscriptio*). Emblems have a tripartite structure. Mottoes, which appear at the top of an emblem, are usually written in

Latin as is seen in Geoffrey Whitney, but George Wither's and Thomas Combe's emblems have mottoes written in English couplets. Pictures follow mottoes. Emblem pictures convey moral meanings allegorically. These meanings are sometimes hard to understand because of their abstraction and conventionality. Emblem poems explain the highly symbolic meanings of emblem pictures. Albrecht Schöene, a German emblem theorist, comments on the interpretive function of emblem poems:

> . . . it [*pictura*] represents directly, in a graphic way, that which will then be interpreted by the emblematic *subscriptio*, in that the latter makes manifest the *significatio* which is contained in the *pictura* and which transcends the *res picta*. Thus every emblem is a contribution to the elucidation, interpretation, and exposition of reality.[3]

Since emblems are pictorial representations, they are static rather than dynamic. That emblems are intended to instruct the reader is explicitly expressed on the title page of Geoffrey Whitney's *Choice of Emblemes, and other Devises* (Leyden, 1586):

> A worke adorned with varietie of matter, both pleasant and profitable: wherein those that please, maye finde to fit their fancies: Bicause herein, by the office of the eie, and the eare, the minde maye reape dooble delighte throughe holsome preceptes, shadowed with pleasant deuises: both fit for the vertuous, to their incoraging: and for the wicked, for their admonishing and amendment.[4]

Emblems are also intended to entertain. It is worth noting that allegorical meanings are pervasive in the Renaissance emblems. In this study I use "allegory" as a general term which is nearly equivalent to symbol.

Taking into account the fact that Renaissance iconography found a way to represent almost every abstraction in pictorial forms, it is not difficult to reason that both of them are closely interlinked with each other. Emblems are iconographical. In other words emblems are pictorial representations of given subjects.[5] For this reason in this study emblem includes iconography even though it needs to be applied only to emblem literature in a strict sense of the word. As Peter Daly notes, emblem is rather a comprehensive term and applies to various forms of art such as painting, carving, and tapestries.[6]

The term "emblematic" needs to be carefully distinguished from emblem. In this study "emblematic" is not used merely as an adjectival form of emblem. It has special implications. While emblem scenes recreate on the stage emblems found in emblem books, emblematic ones indicate those which Shakespeare devised by modifying or adapting the emblems available to him. The playwright might be confronted with occasions where he could not serve his purposes with extant emblems and for this reason needed to modify them. This is not to say that the playwright created his own emblems by looking for emblematic material as Andreas Alciatus ransacked the Greek mythology for the purpose of inventing new emblems. Rather, the playwright drew on the collections of emblems to which he had access. By working on currently circulating emblems the playwright invented some images or concepts which he included in his plays. In brief, emblem scenes are direct borrowings, whereas emblematic ones are his adaptations of emblems in emblem books. In spite of this, it is not always possible to distinguish emblem and emblematic scenes. Emblem traditions in the Renaissance are so complex and composite that it is a delicate thing to decide whether certain images or symbols are direct borrowings or innovations. Nevertheless, this fact does not affect my study since my focus is on the moral and ethical meanings of the scenes and their function, and not on their distinction.

One additional comment. Emblematic scenes may suggest

the assumption that such scenes are abstruse because they are Shakespeare's personal adaptations. However, the fact that they are the playwright's private adaptations does not mean that they are his personal associations like the symbols in W. B. Yeats's *Vision*. Rather, they are modifications of familiar contemporary emblems. This explains why they are communicative to the audience of the Renaissance. Because he must communicate his ideas to the audience, it is hardly conceivable that the playwright would use highly complicated private symbols unless he had a special intention to do so.

In order to discuss the use of emblems to direct and control audience response, we need to pay attention to the differences in the modes of representation between a play and an emblem. In a play the audience watches and listens to actors, whereas a reader looks at and reads an emblem. The audience exploits both the auditory and visual senses in watching a play, but a reader depends only on the visual one. Therefore, in introducing emblems into the theater, the playwright represents the picture of an emblem through actors' actions, except for some cases where special stage machinery can be used. Because of these differences in the modes of representation between an emblem and a play, there can be three possible ways to adapt the former to the latter.

First, playwrights can introduce emblems through the speeches of his characters without presenting them visually by their actions. This auditory delivery is the most common method of using emblems on the stage. However, the audience may not catch the auditory presentation of emblems because sometimes this adaptation results in highly imaginative and poetic imagery. We can find an example of an auditory emblem in II.ii of *Pericles*. In the triumph scene, or festive pageantry, six knights' heraldic devices are orally delivered by Thaisa and Simonides. The device of the fifth knight is "an hand environed with clouds, / Holding out gold that's by the touchstone tried" (II.ii 36-37).[7] This familiar device, whose motto is *Sic spectanda fides* ("So is faith to be tried"), is seen both in Whitney and P. S. P. S. explains the device in Emblem 213:

> The goodnes of gold is not onely tryed by ringing, but also by the touchstone: so the triall of godlines and faith is to bee made not of wordes onely, but also by the action & performance of the deedes.[8]

The second way of using emblems on the stage is to show emblems purely through the actions of actors without speeches or by using some machinery. The Renaissance dumb shows frequently take on the aspect of visual emblems. In *The Tempest* the banquet scene, which Alonso calls "excellent dumb discourse" (III.iii 38), falls into the category of the visual emblem. In *Henry VIII* Shakespeare introduces pageantry which can be termed visual emblems. Performing visual emblems demands great theatrical ingenuity because they are presented only visually without the aid of the rhetorical element.

The third way is to show pictures through actors' actions and poems through their speeches. Storm scenes in *Pericles* and *The Tempest* provide examples of this adaptation. In the tempests enacted in those plays characters' speeches with stage effects and gestures together produce emblems on the stage.

The effect of emblems upon readers is analogous to the effect of theater emblems upon an audience. With regard to the former question, the fact that emblems consist of "silent poetry" (picture) and "speaking picture" (poem) calls for our attention.[9] Poetry is a speaking picture and painting silent poetry. Silent poetry and speaking picture are organized spatially in emblems. The two elements of picture and poem remain separate, though complementary. In addition, emblems mainly appeal to the reader's sight.[10] The reader's act of looking at the picture and reading the poem is largely conducted by his sight. The reader's eyes move back and forth between the picture and the poem when he views emblems. The reader's oscillation between silent poetry and speaking picture mostly arises from the difficulty of comprehending the allegorical and symbolic meanings of the former. The reader, who cannot reach the implicit meaning of the picture, puzzles over it, aided by the poem. The function of symbolic and allegorical images in emblems is to provoke the reader's contemplation, as is pointed out by Christophoro Giarda, a seventeenth-century Italian rhetorician:

> The Symbolic Images, however, present themselves to contemplation, they leap to the eyes of their beholders and through the eyes they penetrate into their mind, declaring their nature before they are scrutinized and so prudently temper their humanity that they appear to the unlearned as masked, to the others however, if they are at least tolerably learned, undisguised and without any mask.[11]

The verbal imagery contained in the poem explains what the reader cannot comprehend in seeing the picture. In this way picture and poem interact with each other in attracting the reader's attention and in provoking his contemplation.

In "To the Reader" George Wither takes note of the contemplative function of emblems as follows:

> For, when levitie, or a childish delight, in trifling Objects, hath allured them to looke on the Pictures; Curiositie may urge them to peepe further, that they might seeke out also their Meanings, in our annexed Illustrations; In which, may lurke some Sentence, or Expression so evidently pertinent to their Estates, Persons or Affections, as well (at that instant or afterward) make way for those Consideration, which will, at last, wholly change them, or much better them, in their Conversation.[12]

Wither's comment tells us about the psychological process of the emblem reader. It also provides an interpretive framework for the last plays. As Wither comments on his "pictures," at first glance the last plays seem to take care of "trifling objects" like fairy tales or children's stories. However, the audience may soon realize the ethical and moral imports of the seemingly simple and trifle stories of the plays. For instance, as the audience keeps watching *Pericles*, it may be convinced of its allegorical and literal dimensions. From a literal perspective the play deals with the adventures of Pericles. From an allegorical perspective it expounds philosophical and moral questions concerning fate and providence, and good and evil. This is also true of *The Winter's Tale*, whose triviality is in fact suggested in the title itself. However, in the course of performance the audience may grasp allegorical meanings. More importantly, the last plays do not impose certain ethical or moral teachings on the audience. As the reader reacts to emblems differently according to his "Persons," "Estates," and "Affections," the last plays offer a wide variety of interpretations. It seems that through emblems the playwright aims to trigger the same effects on the audience as emblems do on the reader.

Both Giarda and Wither lay the groundwork for formulating the relationship between emblems in theater and the audience response. Unlike the reader who depends largely on his eyes in looking at emblems, the audience uses both its eyes and ears. The audience responds to actors' actions, conceived to create visual emblems, with its eyes, and to actors' speeches, conceived to explain the visual, with its ears. Another difference between emblems per se and theater emblems is that the latter are organized temporarily. The temporal organization makes theater emblems more complicated and subtle than literary ones. The playwright can show visual elements and then verbal ones, or reverse this order, or present them almost at the same time. The correlational operation of sight and hearing varies in each case. In other words theater emblems are more dynamic than literary ones. The audience strives to discover the moral and ethical imports lurking behind allegorical and symbolic emblem and emblematic scenes on the stage by activating both its ears and eyes. The audience simultaneously operates its sight and hearing in order to contemplate what it finds enigmatic. Actors' actions and speeches appeal to the audience as a whole, not as separate entities. The minds of the audience move back and forth between its ears and eyes to disclose the moral and ethical imports of what they watch. The audience's exercise of sight and hearing enables it to catch the playwright's messages embedded in given dramatic moments which proceed along the line of time. Unlike the emblem reader who can spend as much time as he pleases on interpreting emblems, the audience needs to succeed in comprehending during a comparatively short time, and this can be possible because of its simultaneous use of sight and hearing.

One of the vital phenomena happening during this psychological process of interpreting emblems is the effect of instructing morality through pleasure. This effect is the aim of emblem literature and Shakespeare applies it to drama. In the course of reading emblems the reader is provided with the ethical and moral lessons in them. The lessons are designed to encourage the reader to practice virtues and eschew vices. This didactic process, however, is carried out in a pleasure-giving way. In "To the Reader" Wither repeatedly stresses this double function of emblems:

> In these Lots and Emblems, I have the same ayme which I had in my other Writings: and though I have not dressed them sutably to curious Fancies, yet, they yield wholesome nourishment to strengthen the constitution of a Good-life; and, have solidity enough for a Play game, which was but accidentally composed; and, by this Occasion.

Giarda presents the same idea as Wither:

> For, by the faith of heaven and of man, is there anything which could demonstrate the power of these excellent faculties more convincingly, which could serve as sweeter recreation and move us more profoundly than this very learned use of Symbolic Images with its wealth of erudition?[13]

It is obvious that the playwright intends to fulfill the instructive and entertaining functions of literature through emblem and emblematic scenes in the same way that poetry does, as Sidney points out:

> Poesy therefore is an art of *mimesis*—that is to say, a representing, counterfeiting, or figuring forth (to speak metaphorically, a speaking picture), with this end, to teach and to delight.[14]

The fact that emblems stimulate contemplation helps us to understand how the playwright manipulates audience response through emblems in the theater. The audience's act of contemplation distances it from the playworld they are engaged in. An audience is engaged in emblem and emblematic scenes but it also contemplates the scenes and is thereby detached as well as involved. In order to catch what the playwright purposes to address through emblems, the audience needs to keep itself at a distance. To put this in another way, the audience temporarily detaches itself from the playworld it is involved in and assumes the role of an observer. If the audience commits the mistake of taking emblem and emblematic scenes at face value, it misses the playwright's important messages for it. At least while the audience is actively engaged in detecting the allegorical and symbolic meanings of what it watches, it remains more separated, detached, and contemplative than emotive, identified, and involved.

This raises the question of why the playwright purposes to

detach the audience, especially in the last plays. One possible answer is that the playwright intends the last plays to be more nonmimetic and symbolic than realistic. In Shakespeare's tragedies, which stand closer to mimetic plays than to nonmimetic, the audience remains more attached to them than detached because of similarity between the audience world and the playworld. However, in the last plays, where nonmimetic elements are stronger than mimetic ones, the audience more often takes the stance of detachment or separation than it does of involvement and identification because of the wide discrepancy between the playworld and the audience world. What the audience sees does not necessarily match what it knows and experiences.

In the last plays there are many unrealistic scenes such as restorations and theophanies. For instance, in the resurrection of Hermione in *The Winter's Tale* and the appearance of Diana in *Pericles*, the audience needs to understand their allegorical or moral meanings instead of just remaining awe-stricken at the spectacles.

At this point it is useful to briefly examine the theory of mimesis or fiction developed by Philip Sidney in order to understand the question of why the playwright intends to produce the effect of detachment on the part of the audience. Sidney defines poesy as an art of imitation. Here imitation is not a photographic reproduction of the world. Rather, imitation is a representation in the poet's imagination or ideas of the world. There are two ways to represent the poet's idea of the world: mimetic and nonmimetic. The mimetic representation is more like a portrayal of the world, while the nonmimetic one is the poet's creative transformation or interpretation of the world. Sidney explains this:

> For any understanding knoweth the skill of each artificer standeth in that idea or fore-conceit of the work, and not in the work itself . . . . which delivering forth is not wholly imaginative, as we are wont to say

by them that build castles in the air; but so far substantially it worketh, not only to make a Cyrus, which had been but a particular excellency as nature might have done, but to bestow a Cyrus upon the world to make many Cyruses, if they will learn aright why and how that maker made him.

According to Sidney every poet produces his work of art based on his "idea" or "fore-conceit." In this sense a poet makes his works out of his "idea" or "fore-conceit" instead of creating out of nothing. He can portray both the historical and particular Cyrus who had been, and the exemplary and ideal Cyrus who had not been. In the former case a poet only needs to work on his present idea about the hero, but in the latter case he needs to bring forth his new idea about him. The former fiction is mimetic in that it touches upon what is or was. On the other hand, the latter fiction is nonmimetic in that it deals with what is not there, but what is invented by the poet. It is dangerous and often impossible to categorize plays according to Sidney's dichotomous classification, since in many cases they are a blend of the two kinds of fictions. However, in terms of Sidney's distinction between these two kinds of fiction, Shakespeare's last plays lie closer to nonmimetic than to mimetic representation. Nonmimetic representation does not treat possible ordinary worlds. In many cases there are logical and psychological gaps between the playworld and the audience world. Since the playwright apparently aims to underline the gaps, he does not attempt to force the audience to accept the plays as mimetic. Rather, he seems to detach the audience from the playworld so that it may use its aesthetic distance to pay attention to something beyond what it sees.

Here arises the question of what kind of lessons the playwright wants the audience to contemplate by detaching it from the playworld. In the following chapters, every effort will be made to discover the moral and philosophical questions Shakespeare purposes to deliver to the audience through emblem and emblematic scenes. The following is a general and brief sketch of the questions.

The relationship between fortune and providence is one of major questions the playwright deals with through theophanies. Providence is purposeful, beneficent, and restorative while fortune is purposeless, malignant, and destructive. The theme of *fortitudo* and *patientia* is also pervasive in the last plays. This moral question embedded in the popular tempest emblem is closely related to the philosophical question of fortune and providence. Those who practice the virtues of patience and fortitude are finally blessed by providence in their voyage in this world which seems to be under the rule of fortune. The relationship between lust / chastity or reason / passion poses another significant moral question. Lust and passion are condemned because they destroy individuals and communities. Chastity and reason are affirmed and commended as personal and societal moral virtues. Besides these questions, the playwright sheds light on moral questions such as faith and time, and political issues such as divine right and harmony, and peace.

Notes

1. Peter Daly, *Literature in the Light of Emblem* (Toronto: U of Toronto P, 1979), p. 185.

2. The six emblem books are: *Jan van der Noot, Theatre for Worldlings* (London, 1569); Samuel Daniel's translation of *The Worthy Tract of Paulus Jovius* (London, 1585); Geffrey Whitney, *A Choice of Emblemes and other Devises* (Leyden, 1586); P. S.'s translation of *The Heroicall Devises of M. Claudius Paradin* (London, 1591); Andrew Willet, *Sacrorum emblematum centuria una* (London 1592?); and Thomas Combe, *Theater of Fine Devices* (London, 1593?). (Peter Daly, ed., *The English Emblem and the Continental Tradition*, p. 52 note 1).

3. Quoted in Peter Daly, *Literature in the Light of Emblem*, pp. 39-40.

4. All quotations in this text from Whitney are from Henry Green, ed., Whitney's *Choice of Emblemes* (London: Lovell Reeve, 1866). This edition was reissued in 1971 by G. Olms in New York and in 1967 by Benjamin Blom in New York. Other editions include Geoffrey Whitney, *A choice of emblemes and other devises* (Amsterdam: Theatrum Orbis Terrarum, 1969; New York: Da Capo Press, 1969) and Geoffrey Whitney, *A choice of emblemes*, 1586, ed. John Horden (Menston: The Scolar Press, 1969).

5. Iconography also denotes the study of "the subject matter or meaning of works of art" (Erwin Panofsky, *Studies in Iconology* [New York: Harper and Row, 1962], p. 3).

6. Peter Daly, ed., *The English Emblem and the Continental Tradition* (New York: AMS, 1988), pp. 1-34.

7. All quotations from Shakespeare are from Alfred Harbage, ed., *William Shakespeare: The Complete Works* (New York: Viking, 1969).

8. P. S., *Heroical Devises . . . of M. Claudius Paradin*, 1591 (Delmar, New York: Scholars' Facsimiles and Reprints, 1984).

9. These are Simonides's terms. Horace's dictum is *ut pictura poesis* (Rosemary Freeman, *English Emblem Books* [New York: Octagon, 1972], p. 14).

10. Peter Daly underlines the precedence of picture over poem: "It follows that the *pictura* is central and primary in that the reader perceives the picture first" (*Literature in the Light of Emblem*, p. 40).

11. Quoted in Ernst H. Gombrich, *Symbolic Images: Studies in the Art of the Renaissance* (London: Phaidon, 1972), pp. 145-46.

12. George Wither, *A Collection of Emblemes*, 1635, ed. John Horden (Menston: The Scolar Press, 1968). All subsequent references in this text to Wither are to this edition. For other editions, see George Wither, *A collection of emblemes, ancient and moderne* (Zurich: Inter Documentation Co., 1969 or 1971); George Wither, *A collection of emblemes, ancient and moderne* (1635), intro. Rosemary Freeman (Columbia, S. C. : U of South Carolina P, 1975).

13. Quoted in Gombrich, *Symbolic Images*, p. 146.

14. All references to Sidney in this text are to Philip Sidney, *A Defence of Poetry*, ed. J. A. Van Dorsten (Oxford: Oxford UP, 1966).

CHAPTER 2

Pericles

Pericles is characterized by the fact that it contains more
emblem scenes than any of the other last play and possibly than
any other play of Shakespeare. The playwright is deeply
steeped in the traditional emblems of his times. Through them
the playwright raises important moral and ethical questions
which form the thematic backbone of the play. These questions
include the relationship between fortune and providence and
the relationship between appearance and reality. The play also
embraces the themes of patience, hope, and time.

The triumph scene, or festive pageantry, in II.ii provides a
good example of emblem scenes in *Pericles*. Simonides, the
king of Pentapolis and Thaisa, his daughter, host the triumph
which is held to celebrate her birthday. In the triumph six
knights appear with shields on which devices and mottoes
are inscribed: the knight of Sparta with the shield of the
black Ethiopian reaching the sun; the prince of Macedon
with the shield of an armed knight conquered by a lady; the
knight of Antioch with the shield of a wreath of chivalry; the
fourth knight with the shield of a burning torch turned upside
down; the fifth knight with the shield of an hand enthroned
with clouds, holding out the gold that is tried by the

touchstone; Pericles with the shield of a withered branch that is green only at top.

Many scholars, for instance, Henry Green, have attempted to identify the devices. Green concludes that "after considerable research through above 20 different books of emblems preceding the time of *Pericles*, I have met with none containing the device of the first and the sixth knight: and we may assign these to Shakespeare's own inventions."[1] Unlike Green, I claim that Pericles's device might be derived from the emblem traditions of the Renaissance even though it is not possible to identify the emblem which exactly corresponds to it. Given the fact that the playwright altered emblems in one way or another in introducing them into the play, it is often, though not always, frustrating to ascertain the iconographic sources of emblem scenes in his plays. It is not at all easy to decide the iconographic sources of emblem scenes in drama because of the many complicating factors in the emblem tradition itself and in its relation to drama.

I propose that Pericles's device is possibly derived from the emblem tradition as a result of comparing it to Wither's emblem 217 (Plate 1). Even though their mottoes are different (Pericles: "*In hac spe vivo* [In this hope I live]); Wither: "*Insperata floruit*" [unexpected flower]), they present almost the same pictures. Moreover, their morals show striking similarities to each other. Simonides offers the moral of Pericles's device as follows: "From the dejected state wherein he is / He hopes by you his fortune yet may flourish" (II.ii 46-47). The epigram of Wither's emblem echoes Simonides:

> T' is true, *a wither'd branch* I am, and seeme
> To some, as voyd of *Hopes*, as of esteeme;
> For, in their judgements, I appeare to be
> A sapless *Bough*, quite broken from the Tree,
> (Ev'n such as that, in this our *Emblem*, here)

And, yet, I neither feele *Despair*, nor *Feare*;
. . . .
  And, what if all who know mee, see me dead,
Before those *hopes* begin to spring and spread?
Have therefore they that hate me, cause to boast,
As if mine expectations I had lost? (1-6, 19-22)

Both Pericles's and Wither's emblems offer a man-tree metaphor. A man in hope is like a flourishing branch and a man without hope is analogous to a withered one. The analogy of man to a tree is not new to the audience who remembers the king of Antiochus's speech in the beginning of the play: "Yet hope, succeeding from so fair a tree / As your fair self, doth tune us otherwise" (115-16). The king of Antiochus argues that he does not want to put Pericles to death because of his hopefulness though he is bound to die because of his misinterpretation of the riddle.

In comparing Pericles's device and Wither's emblem, I do not mean that the latter is the source of the former. Wither's emblem book was published in 1635. It was a general practice that emblem writers collected or compiled emblems rather than produced their own. In this light it is assumed that Shakespeare and Wither were familiar with the withered branch emblem which the latter included in his collection. Wither may have borrowed it from Gabriel Rollenhagen's *Nucleus emblematum selectissimorum* (Utrecht, 1611? or 1613), assumed to be his source, or some other unknown sources.

Pericles's device and Wither's emblem are concerned about hope. Pericles holds on to the hope of rising again to his prosperity from his dejected state. The moral of hope is reinforced by the color symbolism of green. The latter part of Wither's emblem makes reference to the symbolism, too:

No sure: For, I, who by *Faith's* eyes have seene,
Old *Aarons* wither'd *Rod* grow fresh and greene;

And also viewed (by the selfe same Eyes)
Him, whom that *Rod*, most rightly typifies,
Fall by a shamefull *Death*, and *rise*, in spight
Of *Death*, and *Shame*, unto the glorioust *height*. (23-28)

Based on the biblical story of Aaron's rod, Wither regards
green as the symbol of resurrection from death. Hope rests
on the idea that resurrection comes after death. Since it is not
certain whether Shakespeare had the Christian idea of hope
in the color symbolism of green, it is safer to say that the
playwright offers the general idea of hope in it. Andreas
Alciatus, who presents several emblems on hope in his
Emblemata (Lyons 1551), underlines that green is the color
of hope:

Green (viridis) teaches us to hope,
Hope (spes) is said to be vested
In green, no matter how many times it is disappointed. (Emblem
118. 5-6)

What goddess (dea) is this looking up with joyful countenance at
the stars (sidus)?
By whose brush was her image made?
'The hands of Elpidius made me.
This is what I am called:
good hope (Spes) who offers prompt help (ops) to the wretched
(miserus).'
Why is your garment (palla) green (viridis)?
'Because all things flourish (verno) under my leadership (dux).' [2]
(Emblem 44. 1-6)

In Emblem 44 Alciatus provides attributes of hope such as
green, a bow, a cask, and a crow. Hope is represented as a
female figure, dressed in green, with a bow in the left hand,
and sitting on a cask on which a crow perches. In Hertel's
edition of Ripa's *Iconologia* hope is personified as "a
beautiful woman, robed in transparent stuff, with a cloak of
green, and wearing a wreath of flowers on her head." [3]

The moral and philosophical function of Pericles's device lies in its throwing light on the themes of hope. It is hope which sustains Pericles when he undergoes trials and sufferings. It is this hope which enables the prince of Tyre to court Thaisa instead of falling into despair: "This day I'll rise, or else add ill to ill" (II.i 162). He has the hope of rising to his fortune. He runs the risk of wooing Thaisa based on this hope. At least until Pericles is deceived by Dionyza in IV.iii, he acts on hope rather than on despair. Pericles remains courageous and invigorated even after suffering from the two storms which devastate his life.

Pericles's conversation with the fishermen of Pentapolis highlights the hope which sustains Pericles after the first destructive storm. Importantly he expresses his hope through an emblem image. He compares himself to a tennis ball:

> A man, whom both the waters and the wind
> In that vast tennis court have made the ball
> For them to play upon, entreats you pity him. (II.i 58-61)

This emblem image seems to moralize the helplessness of man under the power of nature. However consulting with emblem books, for instance, Wither's, provides a different interpretation. In his emblem 16, whose motto is "When to suppresse us, Men intend, / They make us higher to ascend," Wither clarifies that a tennis ball symbolizes hope:

> WHen we observe the *Ball*, how to and fro
> The *Gamesters* force it; we may ponder thus:
> That whil'st we live we shall be played with so,
> And that the *World* will make her *Game* of us.
> *Adversities*, one while our hearts constraine
> To stoope, and knock the Pavements of Despaire;
> *Hope*, like a Whirle-wind mounts us up againe,
> Till oft it lose us in the empty ayre. (1-8)

As a tennis ball is hit by a tennis player, so man is crushed by adversities. However, man does not stoop to misfortunes but rises again, overcoming despair. Hope supports man in sufferings and enables him to tide over despair. Pericles's device sheds light on the theme of hope which is noticeably underlined throughout the play. That through emblems Shakespeare communicates moral ideas is also clearly seen in the next emblem scene.

The second emblem scene is included in II.iii, where Pericles seems to be impressed by Simonides's kingly features. This scene echoes the traditional iconography of Father Time:

> Yon king's to me like to my father's picture,
> Which tells me in that glory once he was;
> Had princes sit like stars about his throne,
> And he the sun for them to reverence;
> None that beheld him but, like lesser lights,
> Did vail their crowns to his supremacy;
> Where now his son's like a glowworm in the night,
> The which hath fire in darkness, none in light. (37-44)

It seems that Pericles describes a portrait which was in vogue in the Renaissance. However the picture Pericles mentions is not simply a portrait but a kind of emblem. The major reason for categorizing the picture as an emblem, not as a portrait, is that it is concluded by the moral: "Whereby I see that Time's the king of men; / He's both their parent, and he is their grave, / And gives them what he will, not what they crave" (44-46). Moreover, the scene is obviously pictorial, static, and allegorical, which are the main features of emblems. When we interpret the scene only as a portrait, we invite the danger of losing some significant emblematic meanings. In this light I want to pay attention to the phrase, "my father's picture." As many editors have pointed out, the phrase can refer to Pericles's biological father. This interpretation may be true, but it does not explain the reason Pericles mentions Time at the end of his speech. One interesting fact is that in the moral Pericles calls Time the parents of men and men his children. Developing the hero's argument, Time is his father, too. Therefore I suggest that the hero means Time by "my father." Erwin Panofsky observes that Chronos, the Greek name of time, was called "father of all things"[4]

According to Panofsky, three traditions are discernible in the formation of the iconography of Father Time in the Renaissance. In the Middle Ages Time is personified as a bald man with four wings and with a pair of scales or a knife sometimes balanced on two wheels. The bald-headedness of Time reflects the medieval idea of Opportunity. Later in the medieval age the allegorical aspect of Opportunity tended to merge with the figure of Fortune and this results in the image of Time standing on wheels. When the Arab concept of Time as Aion, that is, as "the divine principle of eternal and inexhaustible creativeness,"[5] is conflated with the medieval tradition of Time as Opportunity and Fortune, the picture of Time takes another direction. Time is depicted as a man with a crutch wrapped by the coil of a snake, which represents eternity, and surrounded by the zodiac. The third tradition comes from classical mythology. The similarity between the Greek name of Time (Chronos) and the Greek god, Kronos (Saturn by the Roman name) results in the infusion of qualities such as cruelty and destruction with the medieval and Arabic traditions. In the pictures after the classical tradition Father Time appears nude with a scythe or a sickle instead of a crutch and he does not wear wings.

The image of Father Time in Pericles's speech features an astrological aspect which is thought to be derived from the Arabic tradition. The astrological image of Time enthroned with a crown is not rare in Renaissance art, as is seen in Henry Peacham's *The Gentleman's Exercise . . . in Lymning, Painting, ets.*(1612):

> I haue seen time drawn by a painter standing vpon an old ruine, winged, and with Iron teeth.
>
> But I rather allow his deuise that drew him an old man in a garment of starres, vpon his head a Garland of Roses, eares of Corne and dry stickes, standing vpō the Zodiack (for he hath his strength from heauen) holding a looking glasse in his hand, as beholding onely the present time, two children at his feete, one fat, and well liking, the other leane, writing both in one booke[;] vpon the heade of one, the sunne[;] vpon the other, the Moone.
>
> Hee is commonly drawne vpon tombes in Gardens, and other places an olde man bald, winged with a Sith and an hower glasse.[6]

Peacham mentions that he saw three kinds of iconography of Time, that is, that drawn after the classical, the Arabic, and the medieval traditions. It is the classical tradition to portray Time as a man with iron teeth, though the figure Peacham saw has wings. The old ruin symbolizes the destructive power of Time. The image of Time standing on the zodiac with two sons—the sun and the moon—is obviously modeled on the Arabic tradition. Peacham describes the astrological aspect of time in detail. Lastly Time as a bald man with an hour glass and a scythe is based on the medieval tradition. There are striking similarities between the passage in *Pericles*, "Had princes sit like stars about his throne" (II.iii 39) and Peacham's account, "two children at his feete . . . vpon the heade of one, the sunne[;] vpon the other, the Moone." This noticeable affinities between Pericles's speech and Peacham's account confirms the fact that the former describes the iconography of Father Time.

Identification of Father Time in Pericles's speech is more strongly verified by Panofsky. The art historian remarks that "Time is identified with the Sun" in some iconography including Petrarca's *Triumphus Temporis*.[7] This illuminates the expression in Pericles's speech: "And he the sun for them to reverence" (II.iii 40).

Through the traditional iconography of Father Time

Pericles delivers the glory and majesty of King Simonides as well as the morality of Time. Pericles remembers Father Time at the sight of the king of Pentapolis and it in turn provokes the morals of Time in him. Pericles deeply acknowledges that "He's both their parent, and he is their grave." Here Pericles thinks of Time as "the cosmic universal principle," that is, "a universal and inexorable power which through a cycle of procreation and destruction causes what may be called a cosmic continuity."[8]

As many scholars, for example, Douglas Peterson, have already observed, the thematic implications of Father Time consist in exploring Time as the agent of restoration and destruction.[9] Peterson links the two functions of Time with the two concepts of Time: Time as duration and Time as Occasion. Time as duration causes death and destruction while Time as Occasion produces renewals and recoveries. Based on the two aspects of Time, Peterson concludes that Time can become either the Destroyer or the Renewer according as to how we use it. Chaste love and faith in providence create regeneration, and incest and servility to fortune lead to destruction. Patience and constancy are the two major restorative virtues which empower us to overcome the destructive power of Time. The virtues do not mean passive resignation to the chance of fortune but positive subservience to the purposeful direction of providence. They sustain us in time of adversities and troubles.

Pericles conducts his life according to patience and constancy in Simonides's court. This brings the hero the blessing of his marriage with Thaisa and his recovery of his fortune. He can expect to have an heir who defeats the ruin of time. He recognizes Time as occasion. The emblem scene of Father Time in II.iii conveys these moral and ethical ideas.

Act III Scene i is the third emblem scene. In the scene Pericles appears on the stage and presents the moral of the storm. Considering the fact that the hero's enactment constitutes the picture and his speech the poem of the emblem, the scene is a good example of emblems adapted to the stage. The storm emblem is frequently employed in many emblem books of the Renaissance. For instance, Wither's emblem 37 (Plate 2) explains that man is a boat on the sea of the world and he is required to endure storms of life:

> WEe to the *Sea*, this *world* well compare;
> For, ev'ry Man which liveth in the same,
> Is as a *Pilot*, to some vessell there,
> Of little size, or else of larger frame.
> . . . .
> Each hath proper *Course* to him assign'd,
> His *card*, his *Compasse*, his due Tacklings, too;
> And, if their *Business*, as they ought, they mind,
> They may accomplish all they have to doe.
> . . . .
> Nor, how, *Rash-Lookers* on will censure thee;
> But, faithfully, to doe thy part, assay:
> For, if thou shalt not from this *counsell* vary,
> Let my *Hopes* faile me, if thy Hopes miscarry.

Wither's emblem moralizes the importance of hope which helps us to cope with misfortunes and trials of life. It is human beings who steer the boats of life whether they are barges or argos. Each man is the pilot of life on the sea of the world. Like Wither's emblem 37, Whitney's emblem 137 (Plate 3), whose motto is *constantia comes victoriae* ("constancy is the friend of victory"), concerns the voyage of life on the sea of the world:

> THE shippe, that longe vppon the sea dothe saile,
> And here, and there, with varrijng windes is toste:
> On rocks, and sandes, in daunger ofte to quaile.
> Yet at the lengthe, obtaines the wished coaste:
> Which beinge wonne, the trompetts ratlinge blaste,
> Dothe teare the skie, for ioye of perills paste.

Thoughe master reste, thoughe Pilotte take his ease,
Yet nighte, and day, the ship her course dothe keepe:
So, whilst that man dothe saile theise worldlie seas,
His voyage shortes: althoughe he wake, or sleepe.
    And if he keepe his course directe, he winnes
    That wished porte, where lastinge ioye beginnes.

Like Wither, Whitney compares human life to a voyage on the sea. According to Wither, constancy, that is patience, brings us to the final destination of our voyage in which we confront storms and winds. In this way the storm emblem has a bearing on the theme of patience.

Gower's chorus presents the same analogy of human life to voyage as Wither's and Whitney's:

Their vessel shakes
On Neptune's billow; half the flood
Hath their keel cut: but fortune's mood
Varies again; the grizzled North
Disgorges such a tempest forth
That, as a duck for life that dives,
So up and down the poor ship drives. (III. Chorus 44-50)

Obviously in the passage Gower addresses the emblematic meaning of the storm. The sea is used as a metaphor for fortune or adversity. The human life which is subject to the capricious mood of Fortune is akin to a ship driving up and down on the sea. Man suffers from the inconstancy of fortune when he sails in the world.

Like Wither's and Whitney's emblems, the storm scene in *Pericles* explores the theme of patience. In the scene immediately following Gower's speech Pericles is faced with the birth of Marina, and the seeming death of Thaisa. In the midst of the tragedy of Thaisa's death, Pericles loses his temper to the extent that he blames the gods for it. It is Lychorida who reminds the hero that he should be patient: "Patience, good sir; do not assist the storm" (19); "patience, good sir, even for this charge" (27). When the Tyrian hero listens to Lychorida, he fears the storm no more and has the courage to cast Thaisa into the roaring sea.

Understanding of the moral and philosophical idea of the storm scene is not complete until we direct our attention to the relationship between hope and patience. It is important to notice that Pericles, who vehemently defied the gods, changes so drastically as to call them good: "Now the good gods throw their best eyes upo't . . . . Courage enough. I do not fear the flaw" (37, 39). Pericles's patience and courage stem from his recognition of providence. Pericles seems to be convinced of benign, restorative, and purposeful providence operating behind the apparently destructive and furious storm of fortune. Patience and hope help us to count upon providence, triumphing adversities. It is mistaken, however, to think that *Pericles* centers only on the themes of patience and hope. Through the storm emblem Shakespeare investigates the relationship between fortune and providence as well. In the Renaissance the storm is an emblem of fortune as well as of providence, as Kathleen Williams remarks:

> If the sea is an emblem of dangerous chance, it is also an emblem of the justice of Providence, working through apparent chance itself. The sea washes the armor of Achilles against the tomb of Ajax as it guards and delivers Pericles's wife and daughter, and in Spenser brings Florimell through suffering to new life, and deals absolute justice to the two island-dwelling brothers Amidas and Bracidas in the book of Justice.[10]

A full comprehension of the moral and philosophical meaning of the storm scene calls for a brief examination of the relationship between fortune and providence. According to Leo Salingar, Fortune, or *Fortuna*, which is an important and recurring concept in classical and Renaissance literature, has two distinctive meanings: regularity or cyclic movement and chance or uncertainties.[11] The fact that the term was used in both senses provides a significant clue in probing the relation of fate to providence. It was believed that human life and the world follow certain destined courses according to cosmic principle as seasons that change according to natural principle. From this perspective the courses of human life are fixed and there is no room for freedom or effort. Here the destined courses, however, hint the presence of irrational and malevolent forces controlling human beings. These forces are in opposition to the rational and benevolent associations of providence. Later in the classical period the tradition of fortune as destiny is conflated with that of fortune as chance. Unlike the earlier tradition the later tradition sheds light on the unpredictability and uncertainty of human life and of the world. The illusiveness and trickery of fortune are derived from its uncertainty. Therefore, fate, which could be defined as ordained future, corresponds to the earlier tradition of fortune.

In spite of the fact that fortune seems to be in control of man and the world, providence ultimately shapes them. Divine purpose and rule are the final shaping influence. It is not until providence unfolds its purposes that everything becomes clear and definite. Even if humans and the world seem to be under the power of fortune and thus to be doomed to destruction and decay, it is providence which finally determines them and displays its glory according to its benign purposes. In this sense providence is grace.

On the one hand Pericles, who is driven on the sea of the world, is a victim of "Lady Fortuna" (IV.iv 48). His helplessness and miseries are best exemplified in II.i, where he entreats to "the stars of heaven" for their mercy: "Yet cease your ire, you angry stars of heaven! / Wind, rain, and thunder, remember earthly man / Is but a substance that must yield to you" (II.i 1-3). Pericles acknowledges that he is a passive sufferer in the storm which is unsympathetic to his sufferings. He appears to be astrologically determined to suffer in the sea of the world. On the other hand Pericles is in the control of providence. The grace of providence in opposition to the unkindness of fortune is the invisible driving forces looming behind the hero. In the storm scene of III.i Pericles prays for Neptune's mercy on him:

> The god of this vast, rebuke these surges,
> Which wash both heaven and hell; and thou that hast
> Upon the winds command, bind them in brass,
> Having called them from the deep! (1-4)

He recognizes that nature does not cause a tempest but a god governs it. Pericles is very different from his earlier self, for instance, in the beginning of II.i where he complains against "the stars of heaven," thinking that they are the cause of his misfortune. More importantly, he believes that gods can calm down a tempest. Shakespeare contrasts providential operation and the force of fortune.

George Wither expresses the subtle and mysterious relationship between fate and providence in his emblem 95 (Plate 4), whose motto is "What ever God did fore-decree, / Shall, without faile, fulfilled be":

> ME thinks, that *Fate*, which *God* weighs forth to all,
> I, by the *Figure* of this *Even-Skale*,
> May partly show; and, let my *Reader*, see
> The state, of an *Immutable-decree*;
> And, how it differs, from those *Destinies*,
> Which carnall understandings, doe devise.
>   For this implies, that ev'rything, *to come*,
> Was, by a steady, and by equall *doome*,
> Weigh'd out, by *Providence*. (1-9)

In this emblem Wither draws a scale which represents the ambivalence of fate and providence in life. He ascribes the final outcome of things to providence. Providence is the first principle which operates the world and humans. Through the storm emblem Shakespeare examines the complicated questions of patience and hope on the one hand, and fortune and providence on the other hand. Man, who sails in the sea of the world, is influenced by two opposing forces—*Fortuna* and Providentia. *Fortuna* governs human voyage out of her chance, malignance, and irrationality. Patience preserves humans who are under the merciless rule of *Fortuna*. *Providentia*, however, has her final shaping effects on man. Human destinations and outcomes are ultimately attributed to *Providentia*. Hope is an active virtue which looks forward to *Providentia*. These moral and philosophical imports are eloquently and tacitly passed on to the audience through the storm emblem in the emblem books of the Renaissance.

The fact that Shakespeare was indebted to the emblem traditions of the Renaissance is again borne out by the emblem scene of the Dance of Death in III.ii. The Dance of Death, paintings of which appeared in Paris as early as 1424-1425 in the name of *Danse Macabre*, was brought to perfection in England by Hans Holbein. Together with the storm emblem, the Dance of Death was typical of the iconography popular in the Renaissance Europe.

Shakespeare incorporates the iconography of Dance of Death in III.ii, where Cerimon revives Thaisa from her apparent death. Articulating his motivation in studying nature, Cerimon suddenly inserts the Dance of Death image at the end of his speech:

> I hold it ever
> Virtue and cunning were endowments greater
> Than nobleness and riches. Careless heirs
> May the two latter darken and expend;
> But immortality attends the former,
> Making a man a god. 'Tis known, I ever
> Have studied physic, through which secret art,
> By turning o'er authorities, I have,

Together with my practice, made familiar
To me and to my aid the blest infusions
That dwell in vegetives, in metals, stones;
And can speak of the disturbances
That nature works, and of her cures; which doth give me
A more content in course of true delight
Than to be thirsty after tottering honor,
Or tie my treasure up in silken bags,
To please the fool and death. (26-41)

In the passage Cerimon criticizes the foolishness of people who strive for wealth and honor. He reminds his auditors that they are under the threat of death which destroys human achievements. Plate XLV of 1549 and 1562 editions of Holbein's *The Dance of Death* bears remarkable similarities to Cerimon's image. In the plate the fool holds a bladder in his hand and seems to strike Death with it. Death, however, kicks the fool. This plate obviously satirizes the fool who enjoys his wealth, thinking that he can tread down death. As Hoeniger observes, a Fool and Death are common companions in the Dance of Death.[12]

Shakespeare employs the iconography of the Dance of Death to articulate the philosophical question of art and nature. Cerimon's speech in III.ii is made as an answer to the Gentlemen's question about the relationship between nature and human suffering. In his answer Cerimon underscores "cunning and virtue" which can make a man a god. The Gentlemen attribute human suffering to nature. However, Cerimon argues that human beings can transcend the power of nature and become gods by exercising their reason. They are not born to groan under the cruelty and unkindness of nature which does not seem to be sympathetic with human sufferings. On the contrary they are born to be gods who can exercise control over nature. In this light the true meaning of human life lies in seeking for immortality which can be obtained by exercising reason rather than running after honor or riches.

Human glory and greatness do not lie in riches and honor, but in the employment of nature to cure human troubles. Reason empowers human beings to beat the disasters of nature. Cerimon's immortal fame results from his art of restoring people. His restoration of Thaisa is only one example.

The precedence of art over nature penetrates the whole play. As Cerimon is familiar with physic, so Pericles and Marina are good at dances and songs. In the court of Simonides Pericles professes that he is educated in art and arms: "my education in art and arms" (II.iii 82). However, his art does not cure as many people as Marina's art does. Earlier in his life he almost loses his life by chasing after the daughter of Antiochus out of lust. But his pursuit of the love of Thaisa in the court of Simonides is not influenced by such vices. He has a genuine desire to recover from his present miseries through the marriage with Thaisa. On the other hand, Marina, who "sings like one immortal" and "dances / As goddess-like to her admired lays" (V. Chorus 3-4), revives Pericles from his fatal melancholy and saves Mytilene from the moral corruption which might have brought the wrath of gods as in the case of Antiochus. Cerimon and Marina are two major restorative agents in the play. Throughout the last plays Shakespeare is concerned about the virtuous and restorative use of art.

The fact that Shakespeare is indebted for moral ideas to emblems is further confirmed by V.iii of *Pericles*. This scene contains a harpy emblem. In the scene Cleon, conversing with Dionyza, is startled by her plan to have Marina killed. More surprisingly, she tells that she can deceive Pericles by showing him a false tomb and erecting a monument. At this Cleon employs an emblem image to portray his wife's hypocrisy: "Thou are the harpy, / Which, to betray, dost, with thine angel's face, / Seize with thine eagle's talents" (46-48).

Cleon's description is reminiscent of the harpy in Angelo Bronzino's painting called *Allegory of Luxury* (Plate 5), whose date is placed around 1546, in the London National Gallery. In the painting the harpy in a green dress wears a beautiful face but it cannot conceal its fish-like body, lion's or panther's claws, and dragon's or serpent's tail. She offers a honeycomb with one hand while she hides a poisonous little animal in the other. The marked correspondences between Cleon's harpy and that in *Allegory* convince us that the playwright was familiar with the harpy iconography of the times. Harpies recur in the Renaissance English Literature. In *The Faerie Queene* Spenser describes "Errour" as a monster which has the body of a woman and the tail of a serpent (I.14). The monster is undoubtedly a harpy. The appearance of Ariel as a harpy in III.iii of *The Tempest* is another indicator of the vogue of the harpy.

Panofsky interprets the iconographic meaning of a harpy as follows:

> This [the playful Putto] figure, sometimes described as a Harpy, sometimes, rather inadequately as a 'girl in a green dress,' is unquestionably identical with what Vasari terms *La Fraude*, or deceit. Through it Bronzino manages to give a summary of and almost visual commentary upon the qualities of hypocritical falsehood which are described by sixteenth-century iconologists under such headings as *Inganno, Hippocrisia*, and most particularly *Fraude*. According to the dean of these iconologists, Cesara Ripa, *Hippocrisia* has feet like a wolf, half-concealed by her clothes. *Inganno* can be represented as a woman hiding an ugly face beneath a beautiful mask and offering water and fire 'in alteration.' *Fraude*, finally, is endowed with two heads, one young, one old; she holds two hearts in her right hand and a mask in her left, and she has a dragon's tail, as well as griffon's talons instead of human feet.[13]

It appears to be that Cleon's harpy combines the attributes of *Inganno* ("deception") and *Fraude*. Shakespeare draws on the iconography of the Renaissance to represent Dionyza's deceit. The playwright advises the audience to shun the evil of deceit by appealing to the traditional harpy iconography. The harpy iconography functions to warn the danger of deceit.

In *Pericles* the harpy emblem addresses the moral question of deceit on one hand and the epistemological one of appearance and reality on the other hand. The harpy emblem spells Dionyza's immorality of hypocrisy. Dionyza provokes divine punishment because of her hypocrisy as well as ingratitude, as Gower remarks in his epilogue (11-14). However, the functions of the harpy emblem are not just to deliver moral lessons but to present the philosophical question of appearance and reality. In a sense this question is a framework on which *Pericles* is constructed. Pericles puzzles over this inscrutable and perplexing question from the beginning. When the hero meets Antiochus's daughter, her apparent celestial beauty sweeps him off his feet. But soon the hero is awakened to an unbridgeable gap between appearance and reality: "How courtesy would seem cover sin, / When what is done like an hypocrite, / The which is good in nothing, but in sight" (I.i 122-24). Pericles was naive enough to mistake appearance for reality but comes to realize that beneath the camouflage of courtesy there lurks sin.

In the final act this question of appearance and reality culminates in the reunion of Pericles, Thaisa, and Marina. When Thaisa meets Pericles in Epheseus, she cannot believe what she sees: "O, let me look! If he be none of mine, my sanctity / Will to my sense bend no licentious ear, / But curb it, spite of seeing" (V.ii 28-31). Thaisa will deny the evidence of her senses if Pericles is not his true reality. She is well aware of the discrepancy between appearance and reality. Like Thaisa Pericles cannot believe what he sees. Pericles's disbelief of his sight is grounded on his suffering from deception in much of his life.

The patience emblem in V.i of *Pericles* is the best example
to show how far Shakespeare drew on the emblem traditions
of the Renaissance. I have discussed the moral import of
patience earlier in this chapter in relation to hope. This
section is devoted to a more detailed exploration of the
ethical implications of patience in connection with *fortitudo*.
Moreover the theme of patience was examined previously
under the context of the storm emblem. But in the following
this theme will be dealt with in connection with sculpture. In
the scene where Pericles meets Marina on his ship, he gives a
highly allegorical and symbolic rendering of her image : "yet
thou look / Like Patience gazing on kings' graves and
smiling / Extremity out of fact" (138-40). Pericles's mention
of patience gives a clue to interpreting this passage. He is
possibly describing a personification of Patience. In
Shakespeare, allusion to a personification of Patience occurs
two times—in *Twelfth Night* and *Pericles*. In II.iv of *Twelfth
Night* Viola disguised as Cesario tells Orsino about her
spurious sister and delineates how she behaved when she fell
into love: "She pined in thought; / And, with a green and
yellow melancholy, / She sat like Patience on a monument, /
Smiling at grief" (111-13). *Twelfth Night* and *Pericles* adopt
the same simile, "like Patience," but they differ from each
other in that the former depicts Patience on a monument but
the latter Patience in graves. According to William
Heckscher, the word "monument" is more likely to refer to
two-dimensional representation such as drawing or
illustration rather than to sculpture.[14] In the Renaissance
Patience was commonly personified as a female figure
chained to a rock or a cube which stands for hardships as is
seen in Cesare Ripa's *Iconologia*, where *Patienza*
("patience") is portrayed as a mature woman sitting on a rock
with a mysterious face which can be interpreted either as sad
or as smiling.[15] William S. Heckscher again notes that the

Patience in *Pericles* refers to sculpture rather than to a painting:

> I am thinking of the Fortitudo-Patientia image which we encounter in sculptures of a type that, from the late fourteenth onward, is found attached to regal or princely tombs. Our example (Fig. XIV, Antonio and Giovanni Giusti, "Fortitudo") stems from St. Denis, Paris, where the female figure of "Fortitudo" appears as one of the cardinal virtues adorning the tomb of Louis XII and Anne of Brittany in a setting where the personified virtues, even though they are turned outwards (if seen from their own tomb) are undoubtedly gazing at a vast assembly of other kings' graves.[16]

Heckscher makes two important points. The patience image possibly alludes to sepulchral sculpture. More importantly the concept of patience has close relationship with that of fortitude, which is one of the cardinal virtues.[17] Fortitudo has the double aspects of undertaking dangerous tasks and enduring hardships.[18] The moral significances of the patience image in Pericles's speech, therefore, lie in its highlighting the relation of patience to fortitude. *Fortitudo* is required of man who sails on the sea of life. *Patientia*, which comprises *fortitudo*, is a positive, not a passive, virtue which empowers us to achieve what we desire.

The Patience emblem scene is a thematic nexus which connects the question of patience and fortitude. In the patience emblem scene these themes converge and form a comprehensive and full picture. The emblem scene plays a pivotal role in constructing the themes of the play. Marina is the embodiment of this *fortitudo-patientia* theme. First and foremostly she was born in a storm whose emblematic significance was explained earlier. Moreover, in the course of her life she never falls into despair in a series of events where she is placed under the threat of murder by Leonine, captured by the pirates, and sold to the bawds in Mytilene. Her virtue saved the people of Mytilene. Pericles also owes his revival to Marina's virtue.

Marina's *fortitudo-patientia* is strongly based on her belief in providence. She often prays to gods in her desperate dangers. She entreats to the gods that they may transform her into a bird when she is faced with the violence of Lysimachus: "the gods / Would set me free from this unhallowed place, / Would they did change me to the meanest bird / That flies i'th' purer air" (IV.iv 92-95). Marina's virtue of *fortitudo-patientia* is divine rather than earthly as is implied in *The Tempest*. In the play Prospero claims that Miranda was an angel who protected him from despair: "O, a Cherubin / Thou wast that did preserve me! / Thou didst smile, / Infused with a fortitude from heaven" (I.ii 152-54). Prospero attributes his survival on the sea to the divine fortitude Miranda gave him. The patience emblem links fortitude, patience, and providence.

The theophany of Diana in V.i is the last emblem scene in *Pericles*. The scene is impregnated with moral and philosophical meanings. The ethical and didactic implications in the divine appearance become obvious when we take into account many efforts to moralize the classical mythology in the Renaissance. Classical mythology, which survived through the Renaissance, encountered strong criticism because of its immoral and pagan aspects, which are in opposition to Christian theology. As a result of this classical mythology takes on two directions in order to cope with the charge of obscenity and immorality. Moralization is the effort to proclaim moral truths in the myths. The Renaissance strives to find out a moral allegory in the stories of the Olympian gods. The fact that the moralized *Metamorphosis* went through numerous editions in many European countries proves the preoccupation of the Renaissance people with the moral significances of the myths. In England Arthur Golding and George Sandys produced moralized translations of *Metamorphosis* respectively in 1567 and 1632. Sandys's *Ovid's Metamorphosis Englished, Mythologized, and Represented in Figures* provides the allegorical interpretation.

Diana, the goddess of hunting, represents the virtue of chastity in terms of moral allegory and often the Virgin Mary in terms of Christian theology. The tradition of equating Diana and chastity had been established for a long time. Don Cameron Allen mentions that Diana was called by other names such as Opin, Trivia, Dictynna, and Britomartis.[19] Britomartis, the allegory of chastity in the Third Booke of *The Faerie Queene*, is a variation of Diana. According to Jean Seznec, Diana was interpreted as the Trinity and sometimes as the Virgin Mary in terms of Christian allegory.[20] Henry Hawkins calls Diana the Virgin Mary in Emblem 10 of *Partheneia Sacra*:

> *The Empresse of the Sea,* Latona *bright,*
> *Drawes like a load-stone by attractiue might*
> *The Oceans streames, which hauing forward runne*
> *Calles back againe, to end where they begunne.*
> *The Prince of darknes had ecclipsed* Eues *light,*
> *And Mortals, clowded in Cymmerian night,*
> *Were backwards drawne by* Eue, *as is the Maine;*
> *'Twas only* Marie *drew me to God againe:*
> *O chast* Diana, *with thy siluer beames,*
> *Flux & reflux (as in the Oceans streames)*
> *'Tis thou canst cause O draw! and draw me so,*
> *That I in vice may ebbe, in Vertue flow.*[21]

Hawkins prays to Virgin Mary that she may draw him to virtue away from vice as Latona, the empress of the sea, controls the ebb and flow of the ocean. The emblematist's prayer is constructed on the belief that the Virgin refrains the mankind from falling further by giving them back their lost light, possibly of reason.

The fusion of the moral and the Christian allegories in the theophany of Diana emphasizes the virtue of chastity. Diana and Virgin Mary are the patron goddesses of chastity. Chastity ennobles and glorifies Marina. Marina's chastity brings recovery to Pericles as well as to Lysimachus. Chastity is an agent of both personal and national regeneration. In this light Marina is deified by both Diana and the Virgin Mary because of her chastity as is Miranda by the goddesses—Juno, Ceres, and Iris—in IV.i of *The Tempest.* Marina's chastity forms a foil to the abominable and monstrous incest between Antiochus and his daughter in the beginning of the play. Chastity groups together Marina, Diana, and the Virgin Mary.

On a literal level Diana's appearance evidences providence. The question of providence, which begins to emerge from III.i, is given a final answer. To Marina Diana means the goddess of chastity and to Pericles she is a manifestation of providence. Providence turns out to be benign, restorative, and healing. In a sense all the events converge on this scene and spotlight the theme of providence. Pericles thanks Diana that her appearance confirms him of providence: "Pure Dian, bless thee for thy vision!" (V.iii 69). This tells how the goddess leads Pericles to an insight into the spiritual world. Diana opens the eyes of Pericles to the world of the gods. Diana's appearance assures him of providential operation in his life.

In *Pericles* Shakespeare borrows more emblems directly from the Renaissance emblem traditions than he does in the other last plays. He exploits these emblems as the means of transferring his moral and ethical ideas to the audience. The fact that the play has more emblems than any other last play indicates that the playwright begins to experiment with them in *Pericles.* His experimentation develops into making emblematic scenes out of emblems available to him. His mature craftsmanship to design emblematic scenes is best seen in the plays such as *The Winter's Tale and The Tempest.* In the middle lies *Cymbeline* which I will discuss in the next chapter.

Notes

1. Henry Green, ed., Whitney's *Choice of Emblemes* (London: Lovell. Reeve, 1866), p. 298.
2. All quotations in this text from Alciatus are from Peter Daly, et al., eds., *Andreas Alciatus*, 2 vols. (Toronto: U of Toronto P, 1985).
3. Cesare Ripa, *Baroque and Rococo Pictorial Imagery: The 1758-60 Hertel Edition of Ripa's Iconologia,* ed. and trans. Edward Maser (New York: Dover, 1971), p. 175.
4. Erwin Panofsky, *Studies in Iconology* (New York: Harper and Row, 1962), p. 74.
5. Panofsky, *Studies in Iconology,* p. 72.
6. Quoted in William Shakespeare, *The Winter's Tale,* ed. J. H. Pafford (London: Methuen, 1963) Appendix I p. 167.
7. Panofsky, *Studies in Iconology,* p. 79 note 37.
8. Panofsky, *Studies in Iconology,* p. 82.
9. Douglas Peterson, *Time, Tide, and Tempest: A Study of Shakespeare's Romances* (San Marino, California: The Huntington Library, 1973), p. 14-44.
10. Kathleen Williams, "Spenser: Some Uses of the Sea and the Storm-tossed Ship," *Research Opportunities in Renaissance Drama* 13-14 (1970-71): 137.
11. Leo Salingar, *Shakespeare and the Traditions of Comedy* (Cambridge: Cambridge UP, 1974), pp. 129-56.
12. William Shakespeare, *Pericles,* ed. F. D. Hoeniger (London: Methuen, 1963), p. 87 note 42.
13. Panofsky, *Studies in Iconology,* p. 89.
14. William Heckscher, "Shakespeare in His Relationship to the Visual Arts: A Study in Paradox," *Research Opportunities in Renaissance Drama,* 13-14 (1970-1971): 38.
15. Cesare Ripa, *Iconologia,* p. 381.
16. William Heckscher, pp. 40-41.
17. The four cardinal virtues are *prudentia, justitia, fortitudo. temperantia.* For a more detailed discussion, see Chapter 3.
18. William Heckscher, p. 41.
19. Don Cameron Allen, *Mysteriously Meant: The Rediscovery of Pagan Symbolism and Allegorical Interpretation in the Renaissance* (Baltimore: The Johns Hopkins UP, 1970), p. 221.
20. Jean Seznec, *The Survival of Pagan Gods: The Mythological Tradition and Its Place in Renaissance Humanism and Art* (New York: Pantheon, 1953), p. 93 and p. 266.
21. Henry Hawkins, *Partheneia sacra,* 1633, ed. John Horden (Menston: The Scolar Press, 1971), P.111 All subsequent references in this text to Hawkins are to this edition. Other modern edition is Henry Hawkins, *Partheneia sacra,* intro. Iain Fletcher (Aldington: Hand and Flower Press, 1950).

CHAPTER 3

Cymbeline

Cymbeline features many scenes whose allegorical and symbolic meanings are intimately infused with the literal ones. Another feature of the play is that it is sometimes highly difficult to draw a line between emblem and emblematic scenes. Emblem scenes include the Imogen-Fidele figure who appears from III.vi and the headless man scene in IV.ii. Emblematic scenes consist of the cave scenes in III.iii and III.vi and the vision scene in V.iv. Imogen-Fidele poses the question of faith in relation to suffering and restoration, and the headless man scene presents the moral questions of the relationship between virtues and vices / reason and passion. The cave scenes address the question of personal and social virtues, and the theophany focuses on the question of fortune and providence.

From III.ii Imogen appears not only as a literal figure of a princess of ancient Britain but also as an allegorical figure of "Fidele," representing Faith. Imogen-Fidele acts out the two different roles. Imogen as Faith echoes Marina as Patience in V.i of *Pericles*. The allegory of faith won popularity in the Renaissance emblems. In Hertel's edition of Cesare Ripa's *Iconologia* "Faith" is personified as a woman dressed in white and wearing a helmet. She stands on a low pedestal and reads a book in her hand. In the other hand she holds a light which signifies the illumination of heart by faith.[1] George Wither provides a somewhat different personification of Faith from that of Ripa. In his emblem book Faith is personified as a woman standing on a squared stone with a cross in one hand and a cup in the other hand. The cross and the cup symbolize affliction and comfort respectively. The crown denotes the glory and reward with which the figure is blessed. Henry Peacham offers almost the same picture of Faith as has Wither. Peacham's Faith stands with a book instead of a cup and she leans on a cross.

Shakespeare infuses both the allegorical figure of faith and the character of the Briton princess in Imogen, especially in the second part of the play. This is borne out by the fact that faith constitutes an important theme in the second part. The restorations and reconciliations in the last scene hinge on this theme. It is obvious that the playwright drew on the emblematic image of faith to underscore the thematic relations of the idea to the play.

Wither's "illustration" of Emblem 81 (Plate 6) moralizes faith:

> Hereby, this *Vertue*'s nature may be knowne:
> Now, practise, how to make the same thine owne.
> Discourag'd be not, though thou art pursu'd
> With many wrongs, which cannot be eschew'd;
> Not yeeld thou to *Despairing*, though thou hast
> A Crosse (which threatens death) to be embrac't;
> Or, though thou be compell'd to swallow up,
> The very dregs, of *Sorrowes* bitter *Cup*:
> For, whensoever griefes, or torments, paine thee,
> Thou hast the same *Foundation* to sustaine thee:
> The selfe same *Cup* of *Comfort*, is prepared
> To give thee strength, when *fainting fits* are feared:
> And, when thy *time of tryall*, is expired,
> Thou shalt obtaine the *Crowne*, thou hast desired. (17-30)

The emblematist explores the functions faith performs in our daily life. Faith sustains us in time of trials and sufferings, represented by the cross. It comforts us with "the Cup of Comfort" when we drink up the dregs of the "bitter cup." Finally it prepares us the crown of reward and glory. Faith brings us a final victory.

In Emblem 7 (Plate 7) of his *Minerva Britanna* Henry Peacham also deals with the same theme from a slightly different point of view:

My hope in heauen, the crosse on earth my rest,
The foode that feedes me is my Saviours bloud,
My name is FAITH to all I doe protest,
What I beleeue is Catholique and good,
 And as my Saviour strictly doth commaund,
 My good I doe with close and hidden hand.
Nor Heresie, nor Schisme, I doe maintaine,
But as CHRIST'S coate so my beliefe is one,
I hate all fancies forg'd of humane braine,
I let contention and vaine strifes alone,
 If ought I neede I craue it from aboue,
 And liue with all in Charitie and Loue.[2]

Unlike Wither, Peacham stresses the practical acts of faith which consist of charity and love. He encourages the reader to stay away from vices such as "Heresie" and "Schisme" by putting hope in heaven and resting on the cross. Faith enables us to perform virtuous acts. Peacham's view of faith is more ethical and orthodoxic than Wither's. But the moral and philosophical imports of faith in *Cymbeline* are more closer to Wither's moralization than Peacham's.

In the second part of *Cymbeline* Imogen enters as a kind of pilgrim going to Milford Haven, which has the unmistakable emblematic implications. As a pilgrim figure like "Christian" in John Bunyan's *The Pilgrim's Progress*, Imogen embodies the allegorical figure of faith. Though her allegorical character is subtly commingled with her literal one, Imogen's conversation with Belarius which takes place shortly after she comes on the stage in III.vi reveals her allegorical character:

Belarius	Whither bound?
Imogen	To Milford Haven
Belarius	What's your name?
Imogen	Fidele . . . . (59-62)

In this scene Imogen as faith is outstanding enough to obscure her as a Britain prince. Imogen as an allegorical figure of faith is confirmed when she is asked her name two more times later in the play: "Thy name? / Fidele, sir" (IV.ii 378-79); "What's thy name? / Fidele, sir" (V.v 119-20).

When Imogen appears in III.vi, she is mentally and physically disappointed and weary due to Posthumus's betrayal and her hunger: "I have tired myself, and for two nights together / Have made the ground my bed. I should be sick / But that my resolution helps me" (2-4). It is her "resolution" which sustains her. Her adversity is clearly seen in her confession that she slept on the bare ground for two nights. In this desperate situation she is further tormented by the fear that Jove might abandon her: "O, Jove, I think / Foundations fly the wretched—such, I mean, / Where they should be relieved" (6-8). She is gripped by the fear that Jove deserts wretched people like her who are in need of his salvation. She is on the point of falling into despair thinking that she lacks the "foundations" (security). She groans under the crosses of trials. Imogen in III.vi is a counterpart of the cross Faith carries and embraces in Wither's emblem.

However Fidele is offered a "Cup of Comfort" given by the cave people. The virtues of Belarius, Arviragus, and Guiderius invigorate the lowered spirit of Fidele. As Douglas Peterson remarks in *Time, Tide, and Tempest*, Belarius, Arviragus, and Guiderius show the virtue *of humanitas*, which comprises benevolence, beneficence, and liberality.[3]

Their *humanitas*, which parallels that of Senior Duke in *As You Like It*, comforts the weary and despairing Fidele. Arviragus and Guiderius immediately welcome her by willingly acknowledging her as their brother: "I'll love him as my brother" (III.vi 71). Through the kindness and gentleness of these "kind creatures" (IV.ii 32), she begins to recover from her despair.

Fidele's despair and sorrows, however, are so great that she takes the "confection" to bear them. This stuff, "being tak'n," "would cease / The present pow'r of life, but in short time / All offices of nature should again / Do their due functions" (V.v 255-57). Her taking the stuff corresponds to Faith's drinking the dregs of the "bitter Cup" in Wither's emblem. The medicine leaves her in the apparent death. She is overwhelmed by the death the cross threatens.

Fidele's waking from her coma brings her more crosses to bear because of her mistaking the headless body of Cloten for Posthumus. She has been temporarily diverted from the way to Milford Haven. However her consistent desire to reach there is not thwarted by the faint caused by the potion. The words she speaks right after she wakes reflects this: "Yes, sir, to Milford Haven. Which is the way? . . . Faith, I will lie down and sleep" (IV.ii 291-94). This speech proves her constancy which characterizes faith. Fidele is a faithful pilgrim who keeps going the way to salvation.

Imogen as Fidele sheds light on the thematic role of faith in *Cymbeline*. Imogen is an allegorical figure who embodies the process of suffering, despair, comfort, and reward Faith goes on a pilgrimage. Imogen's faith functions as a major agent of restorations and revivals concluding the last scene of the play. Like the Virgin Mary Imogen symbolizes the unfailing and incorrupt faith of the ancient Britain under the rein of Cymbeline. Faith represented by Imogen is underlined as both personal and national virtue.

The headless man episode in IV.ii does not seem to be an emblem scene until it is discovered that it is indebted to the emblem tradition of the Renaissance. This discovery leads us to the identification of the moral and ethical imports of the scene. These emblematic meanings are closely connected with the literal ones. On a literal level the scene touches the theme of appearance and reality. Imogen's confusion of Posthumus and Cloten spotlights the resemblance of seeming and truth. Imogen's confession eloquently voices this theme: "Our very eyes / Are sometimes like our judgments, blind" (IV.ii 301-2). The unfathomable relationship between "seeing" and "judging" remains a puzzling problem to Imogen as well as to other characters. Imogen is deeply aware of the indistinguishableness of truth and error / dream and life / appearance and reality. The boundary between these different entities is blurred.

The blurred boundary is represented by the headless body which is the conflation of Posthumus and Cloten. The coalescence of the two characters in the headless body triggers additional emblematic meanings in the scene. The scene incorporates two moral imports which are figured forth by the two figures. The headless body signifies the decapitation of Cloten, which is an emblematic representation of the victory of virtue over vice. On the other hand it symbolizes Posthumus's passion as opposed to reason.

Some lines before the headless man episode Guiderius has killed and decapitated Cloten. Guiderius's brutal act of beheading conveys some allegorical imports. According to John Doebler, the decapitated head symbolizes God's punishment of Satan promised in Genesis 3:15: "In all these cases the head of God's enemy is either bruised or cut off."[4] The decapitated head of Cloten expresses the purgation of an agent of evil as does the beheaded one of Macbeth: "Enter Macduff, with Macbeth's head" (V.viii 53).

The equation of Cloten with evils or vices is suggested in the monster imagery Belarius uses in referring to the prince. Immediately after Guiderius shows up with Cloten's head, Belarius responds to Guiderius as follows: "Then one good ground we fear, / If we do fear this body hath a tail / More perilous than the head" (IV.ii 144-45). Belarius describes Cloten as a monster. He fears that the remaining tail of the monster might do the cave dwellers harm. Possibly Belarius means the queen and Cloten by the tail and the head respectively. Cloten and the queen together are symbolically a monster which does evils and vices. They threaten to destroy Britain and virtuous people such as Imogen.

Cloten's threatening of virtues is definitely seen in his intention to kill Posthumus and to rape Imogen. These evils of Cloten's are materialized by an emblematic image. The following citation clarifies this:

> Not Hercules
> Could have knocked out his brain, for he had none. (IV.ii 115-18)

It is possible that Guiderius alludes to the myth of Hercules's fight with Hydra. George Sandys narrates the mythological episode in the "Ninth Booke" of his *Ovid's Metamorphosis*:

> To strangle Serpents was my cradles sport.
> Though other dragons to thy conquest bow:
> To dire Lernean Hydra what art thou?
> Each of her hundred necks two fiercer bred:
> More strong by twining heires. These thus renu'd
> And multiply'd by death, I twice subdu'd.[5] (67-72)

The legend has it that Hercules killed two serpents sent by Juno when he was young. Later he fought with Hydra whose heads multiplied when they were cut off. Sandys comments that Hydra is a kind of water snake which connotes lust or carnal pleasures: "Nor is pleasure and lust unaptly expressed by serpents."[6] The moral of Guiderius's speech quoted above is that he overpowers the vices represented by Cloten as Hercules slew Hydra. The analogy of Cloten to Hydra is extended to that of Guiderius to Hercules who frequently appears an emblematic figure symbolizing virtue in Renaissance Europe. Guiderius's decapitation of Cloten allegorically signifies that virtue has triumphed over vice.

Cloten's lust and enmity stem from his irrationality. His lack of reason prevents him from seeing his true self. In I.ii he thinks of himself as courageous even though he was nearly killed in a duel with Posthumus. In II.i he imagines that his swearing matches his princeship: "and then a whoreson jacknapes must take me up for swearing, as if I borrowed mine oaths of him and might not spend them at my pleasure" (3-5). He boasts about the fact that he can make oaths as well as ordinary people. Cloten's irrationality is, however, best demonstrated by his notion of clothing. He believes that his donning Posthumus's clothing makes him worthy of Imogen's love: "How fit his garments serve me! / Why should his mistress, who was made by him that made the tailor, not be fit too" (IV.i 2-4). Cloten's logic is that Imogen is his suitable marital partner as Posthumus's garment fits him. He does not realize that marital partnership and the fitness of clothing are two different things.

That Cloten lacks reasoning power is poignantly pointed out by Guiderius: "This Cloten is a fool, an empty purse; / There was no money in't" (IV.ii 115-16). He does not even deserve to be treated as a man, let alone a prince. Cloten is a fool who does not have the reason which makes man different from animals. In view of the fact that the Renaissance people identified the head as the seat of reason, Cloten is symbolically said to be a headless man. The fact that he is a headless monster has been already indicated in

Guiderius's speech quoted above: "Not Hercules / Could have knocked out his brains, for he had none."

The head as the place of reason predominates in Renaissance emblems. Geoffrey Whitney documents this in Emblem 229:

WHERE liuely once, Gods image was expreste,
Wherein, sometime was sacred reason plac'de,
The head, I meane, that is so ritchly bleste,
With sighte, with smell, with hearinge, and with taste.
Lo, nowe a skull, both rotten, bare, and drye,
A relike meets in charnell house to lye.

Whitney grieves over the fact that the head, the place of reason, becomes rotten. The skull, which is also a *memento mori* ("remember death"), emblematizes the decay of reason. In Emblem 98 Andreas Alciatus also claims that the head is the seat of reason or virtue:

He is a man (vir) to his loins, because virtue (virtus) implanted in us,
rising in the heart (cor), has its seat in the lofty citadel of the head (vertex),
. . . .
Some attribute wisdom (sophia) to the heart, others to the brain (cerebrum).

Alciatus assumes that virtue or wisdom rises from the heart and remains in the head. Marnef, a sixteenth-century French translator of Alciatus, renders the Latin word *virtus* into *raison* meaning reason:

One honours (honorer) Pan or Nature, a half-goat man (homme), a half-man god (dieu), everywhere. From the navel up, from the heart (coeur) to the head (chef), he is a man for *reason* (raison) rises to the top.[7] (italics mine)

Reason and sexual desire characterize human beings.

Reason, which distinguishes man from animals, is made in the heart and rises up to the head, its seat.

Therefore the image of a headless body derived from the idea of the head as the seat of reason represents the lack of the guidance of reason. Thomas Combe advances this idea in his Emblem XVI (Plate 8) which pictures a headless woman. The emblem, whose motto is "Search for strange monsters farre or wide, / None like the woman wants her guide," presents the following poem:

> Great monsters mentioned are in stories found,
> As was *Chymera* of a shape most wondrous,
> *Girion, Pithon, Cerb'rus* that hel hound,
> *Hydra, Medusa*, with their heads most hideous,
> Satyres and Centaures; all these same were found
> In bodies strange, deformed and prodigious:
>   Yet none more maruellous in stories read,
>   Then is a woman if she want a head.[8]

Man without a head is more monstrous than monsters found in traditional mythologies. Reason is the true guide that leads man to virtuous and noble life. Jean Seznec mentions that "the human head represents Prudence, in the terms of scholastic moral theology."[9] When men are not assisted by the guidance of reason, they bring about tragedies.

Just as important, Cloten is also a parody of Posthumus. Like Cloten Posthumus conducts his life according to passion not reason. Posthumus becomes a headless man in a metaphorical sense. He deteriorates morally. His moral deterioration is caused by Iachimo's implanting doubt in him. In II.iv where Posthumus oscillates between Iachimo and Philario, his judgment is totally influenced by his passion. In spite of Philario's warning against believing Iachimo, Posthumus succumbs to the latter's circumstantial evidence of Imogen's infidelity. This scene is quite reminiscent of *psychomachia*, that is, a medieval allegory of the war between vices and virtues. Posthumus listens to the vicious words of Iachimo instead of the rational and virtuous words of Philario:

> Philario Sir, be patient.
> This is not strong enough to be believed Of one persuaded well of.
> Posthumus Never talk on't.
>   She hath been colted by him.
> Iachimo If you seek
>   For further satisfying, under her breast— Worthy the pressing—lies a mole, right proud
>   Of that most delicate lodging. By my life,
>   I kissed it, and it gave me present hunger
>   To feed it again, though full.

Iachimo arouses Posthumus's jealousy through the sex-food metaphor. Iachimo compares sex to food. To satisfy sexual desire is like filling a hungry stomach. These biological desires have nothing to do with morals or ethics. Being overwhelmed by Iachimo's logic, Posthumus suddenly questions Imogen's integrity and faithfulness. He becomes the prey of sexual jealousy. Like Leontes in *The Winter's Tale*, Posthumus's erupted jealousy keeps him from exercising reason. Love and marriage become detestable to him. To him woman is an animal which seeks only to gratify its sexual desires. Posthumus's speech denouncing womanhood bears similarities to Leontes's speech condemning wives:

> Posthumus Is there no way for men to be, but women
>   Must be half-workers? We are all bastards (II.v 1-2).
> Leontes Should all despair
>   That have revolted wives, the tenth of mankind
>   Would hang themselves. (I.ii 207-9).

Both Posthumus's and Leontes's despair with their beloved wives is so complete that they think that they are cuckolded.

Their disgust with womankind is so strong that they would choose to live single rather than reproduce bastards. Posthumus deplores over bisexual human reproduction as Adam does in Book X of *Paradise Lost*:

> O why did God . . .
> . . . create at last
> This novelty on Earth, this fair defect
> Of Nature, and not fill the World at once
> With Men as Angels without Feminine,
> Or find some other way to generate
> Mankind? (888-95)

Posthumus pursues Imogen to kill her as Leontes imprisons Hermione. Posthumus's intention to murder his wife parallels Cloten's vow to rape and kill Imogen. Both Posthumus and Cloten threaten the life of Imogen. Posthumus falls from his moral integrity and degenerates into a senseless man. Hatred and jealousy drive him to seek for vengeance. He thinks of himself as a devil:

> I'll write against them,
> Detest them, curse them. Yet 'tis greater skill
> In a true hate to pray they have their will;
> The very devils cannot plague them better. (II.v 31-34).

He is full of hatred, vengeance, and curses. He aims at doing harm skillfully. At this moment he parallels Satan in Book IV of *Paradise Lost* who falls a second time by declaring that "Evil be thou my Good" (110).

The fallen Posthumus is nothing better than a headless monster. He is not controlled by reason any more. It is ironic that Imogen cries over the headless body of Cloten, mistaking it for Posthumus's: "O Posthumus, alas, / Where is thy head? Where's that? Ay me, where's that?" (IV.ii 320-21). Imogen ironically suggests the fact that Posthumus is a headless monster.

However, unlike Cloten, Posthumus does not pay with death because of his folly. As Douglas Peterson observes, he recovers from his moral fall through a process of regeneration.[10] His regeneration begins with repentance. His entrance in V.i signals his recovery from his degeneration. He realizes the divine punishment which he incurs by telling Pisanio to kill Imogen. His act of repentance is finally rewarded with the grace of salvation confirmed by the theophany.

Posthumus's moral fall poses a great danger to Britain as well as to Imogen. Seeking to avenge Imogen, he comes over to his fatherland as one of the invading army of Rome. He threatens to defeat his fatherland out of his personal bitterness caused by his mistaken idea of Imogen's chastity. Posthumus, however, contributes to the consolidation of the Briton monarchy along with Belarius and the two princes. Their virtues save Britain from the vices of Cloten and the queen and defend her from the invasion of Rome. As Cymbeline notes, they are the vital parts of the body politic of Britain:

> To my grief, I am
> The heir of his reward, [to Belarius, Guiderius, and Arviragus]
>   which I will add
> To you, the liver, heart, and brain of Britain,
> By whom I grant she lives. (V.v 11-14)

Their courage, wisdom, and reason rescue the body politic.

In summary, the headless man scene touches the punishment of evils, and the relationship between reason and passion in connection with individuals as well as to the body politic. The fact that moral meanings are contained in literal ones is true not only of the emblem scenes discussed above but of the emblematic scenes to be discussed in the following.

The cave scenes in Acts III and IV are emblematic in that

they are not directly indebted to the emblem tradition of the Renaissance Europe but perform the same functions as emblems. As many critics have noted, Belarius provides the perspective to interpret the scenes in his moralization: "To apprehend thus / Draws us a profit from all things we see / And often, to our comfort" (III.ii 17-19). "Profit" means moral edification. Belarius recommends his two sons to look at things from a moral perspective. The scenes are tableaux which convey symbolic or allegorical meanings. The cave is the dwelling place of Belarius, Arviragus, and Guiderius. It also reflects the excellencies and limitations of the virtues of the cave dwellers.

The cave people are exemplars of virtues. According to Adolf Katzenellenbogen, in medieval Christian allegory the virtues are codified in the so-called *Arbor bona*, that is, Tree of Virtues. *Humilitas* is the root, three theological virtues occupy the top, and four cardinal virtues form the trunk of The Tree. Theological virtues consist of *fides, spes, and caritas* whereas cardinal virtues include *prudentia, justitia, fortitudo, and temperantia.*[11] Among the cardinal virtues *fortitudo* and *justitia* are classified as social ones while others as individual ones.

The cave people perform the virtues of *humilitas* and *caritas. Humilitas* is shown in their humble life in the cave. In the beginning of III.iii Belarius underscores their simple and innocent life as opposed to a proud and vain courtly one:

> A goodly day not to keep house with such
> Whose roof's as low as ours! Stoop, boys. This gate
> Instructs you how t' adore the heavens and bows you
> To a morning's holy office. The gates of monarchs
> Are arched so high that giants may jet through
> And keep their impious turbans on without
> Good morrow to the sun. Hail, thou fair heaven!
> We house i'th rock, yet use thee not so hardly
> As prouder livers do. (1-8)

The low roof of the cave indicates its humbleness as the high gate of the court signifies its pride. The cave dwellers' humbleness is seen in their worshiping heaven. In spite of the fact that they live in a low-roofed cave, they live a moral and noble life. Their moral standards are much higher than courtiers.

The cave dwellers' *caritas* is exemplified by their hospitality toward Imogen. They are kind and generous in offering Imogen food. Their kindness corrects Imogen's idea that they are rude and savage: "These are kind creatures. Gods, what lies I have heard! / Our courtiers say all's savage but at court / Experience, O thou disprov'st report!" (IV.ii 32-34). Imogen is awakened to the real kindness of the cave people. Her experience has widened her moral perspective. True kindness and gentility reside not in noble birth and graceful costume but in virtuous actions and honorable character.

The cave people's moral standards and their practice of virtues partially qualify their residence to be an ideal pastoral place where restorations and renewals occur. They make their everyday life a kind of feast, as Belarius comments: "You, Polydore, have proved best woodman and / Are masters of the feast. Cadwell and I / Will play the cook and servant; 'tis our match" (III.vi 28-30). Their cave is not a savage but a happy place as long as they are virtuous. They enjoy a self-sufficient life which is constructed on their virtues as is explained in Andreas Alciatus's emblem 37:

> The poor(inops) Hun, the most miserable dweller near the Scythian Sea(pontus),
> constantly has his limbs pinched lived with cold(gelus).
> He knows not the wealth(ops) of Ceres, nor the gifts(donum) of Bacchus(Lyaeus);
> nevertheless, he always has precious clothing.
> For skins(pellis) of martens(murinus) envelop him on all sides;
> only his eyes are visible, every other part is covered.
> Thus he fears(metuo) no thief(fur), thus he disdains the winds(ventus) and rain-storms(imber).
> He is safe(tutus) among men, and safe among the gods.

In spite of the fact that the Scythian Hun lacks worldly wealth and comforts, he leads a self-sufficient life in the cave. He seems to be poor and miserable by worldly standards, but he is one of the safest and happiest men in the world. He fears neither thieves nor storms. Likewise, Belarius lives happily and safely in the cave with the two kidnapped princes. Belarius's happiness and self- sufficiency qualify the cave to be ideal and paradisiac.

Belarius and his sons are hermits living isolated from human world, figures common in Renaissance literature. In *The Rare Triumphes of Loue and Fortune* (1589) Bomelio is a parallel to Belarius.[12] Bomelio is banished from the court of King Phizantes. He stays in a cave as a hermit, studying magic. Unlike the cave in *Cymbeline*, that in *The Rare Triumphes* forms the place where fantastic events take place. When Hermione cannot get marry Fidelia, who is the princess of Phizantes, he runs away to the cave of Bomelio. In the cave Hermione is informed that he is the son of the hermit. The hermit uses magic to make dumb Armenio, the brother of Fidelia, who sneaks in the cave to fetch her away. Finally, Hermione and Fidelia are reunited with each other. In the same cave Bomelio's madness caused by Hermione's burning his magic books and Armenio's dumbness are healed by the blood spilt from Fidelia.

The Sixth Book of *The Faerie Queene* presents an episode about a hermit who lives in "a little Hermitage" (V.34. 8). Spenser depicts him as follows:

> Therein the Hermite, which his life here led
> In streight obseruance of religious vow,
> Was wont his howres and holy things to bed;
> And therein he likewise was praying now,
> Whenas these Knights arriu'd, they wist not where not how.[13]
>   (V.35 5-9)

The hermit is a kind of monk who keeps religious vows and cultivates his mind. His life of prayer best demonstrates his character. As in *Cymbeline* Spenser's hermit functions as an agent of restorations and renewals. He cures Timias, the squire of Arthur and Serena, the lover of Calidore, of the wounds inflicted by the Blatant Beast. He counsels them to refrain outward senses "from things, that stirre vp fraile affection" (vi.7). The hermit in *The Faerie Queene* is an idealized figure while Bomelio in *The Rare Triumphes* a magical one.

Unlike the anonymous author of *The Rare Triumphes* and Spenser, Shakespeare did not merely inherit the hermit figure but modified it to serve a new dramatic purpose. The playwright stresses the moral excellence of the cave people. But at the same time he illuminates the limitations of their moral virtues. They are laudable in terms of individual virtues such as *humilitas and caritas*. However, they lack social virtues such as *fortitudo* and *justitia*. They are secluded from the things of the world. They need to come out of their cave and return to the court from which Belarius fled with the kidnapped princes of Cymbeline. To Guiderius, the cave is "a cell of ignorance, travelling abed, / A prison, or a debtor that not dares / To stride a limit" (III.iii 33-35). The cave is an emblem of the narrowness and limitedness of the hermit life. The cave constrains Guiderius from experiencing the world as Imogen does.

The cave dwellers reach out to the world outside their cave by participating in the war between Britain and Rome. In the war they fully prove their *fortitudo* and *justitia*. Posthumus is overwhelmed by their feat. They are exemplars of *fortitudo*. Their *fortitudo* strikes wonder into the First Captain: "'Tis thought the old man and his sons were angels" (V.iii 85). Their virtues are more divine than humane.

They go to war not for personal profits but for a national

cause. To hide from the war is not honorable. As Belarius states, they risk their lives for their country:

> No reason I since, of your lives you set
> So slight a valuation, should reserve
> My cracked one to more care. Have with you, boys!
> If in your country wars you chance to die,
> That is my bed too, lads, and there I'll lie. (IV.iv 48-52)

Belarius was reluctant to fight for Britain because of his deep-rooted grudge against Cymbeline. But he decides to lay his life for his country, prevailing over his personal interests and affairs. In this sense the war verifies the cave people's *justitia*.

The cave is an emblem of self-sufficiency where the cave people hold a feast every day but also that of the seclusion and limitedness out of which they need to come. It emblematizes both innocence and "ignorance," which lacks experience. The three characters are required to exercise an active life as well as a contemplative life. Individual virtues must be in a good harmony with social ones.

The theophany in V.iv is a second emblematic scene where Jupiter descends on an eagle in thunder and lightning. The vision is indirectly related to the emblem traditions of the Renaissance. The moral and philosophical significance of the vision is clearly discerned by consulting emblem writers of the Elizabethan times, for instance, George Wither. Wither shows that the theophany of Jupiter concerns the question of virtue and fortune. His Emblem 6 (Plate 9) pictures an eagle bearing a person to the heavens and a man turned upside down on the wheel of fortune which the goddess of fortune turns. His interpretation of the picture articulates the question of virtue and fortune:

> UNhappy men are they, whose Ignorance
> So slaves them to the *Fortunes* of the Time,
> That they (attending on the Lot of *Chance*)

Neglect by *Vertue*, and *Deserts*, to clime
. . . . .
You, then, that seeke a more assur'd estate,
On good, and honest *objects*, fixe your *Minde*,
And follow *Vertue*, that you may a *Fate*
Exempt from feare of Change, or Dangers, finde.
For, he that's *Vertuous*, whether high or low
His *Fortunes* seems . . . . regards it not a haire
. . . . .
  Above all Earthly powres his *Vertue* reares him;
And, up with *Eglets* wings, to Heav'n it beares him.

Wither stresses the fact that virtues triumph over the changes and dangers of the world. Man seems to be under the control of Fortune whose favor is "fickle," but his destiny rests on virtues. Virtues carry man to the heavens with "Eaglets wings." Virtues bring heavenly salvation.

In Renaissance Europe, which saw the popularity of viewing classical mythology from the Christian perspective, Jupiter was often equated with the Godhead as is shown in Mutianus Rufus (1471-1526), the German humanist: "You, since Jupiter, the best and greatest god, is propitious to you, may despise lesser gods in silence. When I say Jupiter, understand me to mean Christ and the true God."[14] As many critics have already observed, *Cymbeline* is more deeply steeped in Christian aspects than any other last play. As is signified in the name of Fidele, the second part of the play has an outstanding trait of Christian allegory. This seems to have bearing on the fact that Cymbeline reigned Britain around the time of Jesus's birth:

Next him *Tenantius* raigned, then *Kimbeline*,
What time th'eternall Lord in fleshly slime
Enwombed was, from wretched *Adams* line
To purge away the guilt of sinfull crime:
· O ioyous memorie of happy time,
That heauenly grace so plenteously displayed. (*The Faerie Queene* II.x 50)

Spenser notes that the time of Cymbeline's government echoes the grace of the incarnation of "th' eternall Lord." G. Wilson Knight arrives at the same conclusion that "We have regarded Jupiter as pre-eminently the Romans' god; but he is, throughout Shakespeare, more than that, and may often be best rendered 'God'."[15]

The ghosts in the vision scene raise the question of providence and fortune. Surrounding Posthumus who has fallen into sleep, they present the question to the greatest god. Reviewing the past life of Posthumus, they strongly call into question the divine control of human affairs. Sicilius charges the god with neglecting his duty to perform divine justice. His charge is why the innocent Posthumus undergoes the trials and sufferings: "Whose father then, as men report / Thou orphans' father art, / Thou shouldest have been, and shielded him / From this earth-vexing smart" (V.iv 39-42). Sicilius argues that Jupiter does not care for Posthumus though he is the god of orphans, a trait often mentioned of Jehovah in the Prophets of the Old Testament. Some lines later Sicilius continues to blame the god for Posthumus's deception by Iachimo:

> Why did you suffer Iachimo,
> Slight thing of Italy,
> To taint his nobler heart and brain
> With needless jealousy,
> And to become the geck and scorn
> O'th' other's villainy? (63-68)

According to Sicilius, Jupiter allows Iachimo to tempt Posthumus and leads the latter to become the prey of the "needless jealousy." Sicilius's idea of divine control does not allow for human freedom. He insists that he is entirely responsible for the fall of Posthumus.

In contrast with Sicilius, the brothers ask the god to show

graces on him, who is in extreme sorrow, by considering the
fact that he was meritorious and virtuous : "Why hast thou
thus adjourned / The graces for his merits due, / Being all to
dolors turned?" (78-80). They appeal to the grace of Jupiter
for the redemption of Posthumus. They argue that Posthumus
needs Jupiter's salvation and entreats the god's speedy
intervention. They emphasize that he was an unparalleled
man in dignity and maturity, as was judged by Imogen:

> When once he was mature for man,
>   In Britain where was he
> That could stand up his parallel,
>   Or fruitful object be
> In eye of Imogen, that best
>   Could deem his dignity? (52-57)

The brothers imply that Posthumus was virtuous though he
has fallen and call for the divine mercy on him. As explained
in Wither's emblem, they believe that Posthumus's virtues
destroy the operation of fortune. His virtues would rear him
up from his miseries.

The ghosts, who are a parallel to the chorus in the Greek
tragedies, raise the fundamental question of divine control
and human fortune. Jupiter gives an authentic answer to this
question which is possibly asked by Posthumus himself and
the audience, as well:

> Whom best I love I cross; to make my gift,
>   The more delayed, delighted . Be content.
> . . . .
> He shall be lord of Lady Imogen,
>   And happier much by his affliction made.
> This tablet lay upon his breast, wherein
>   Our pleasure his full fortune doth confine. (101-2, 107-10)

Jupiter responds that providence controls Posthumus's
fortune. Jovial providence aims at the hero's restoration and

beneficence. Through his trials Posthumus will be happier ("the more delayed, delighted"). Moreover, providence is purposeful. Jupiter purposely delayed his "gift" to augment Posthumus's joy. The inscrutable relationship between Posthumus's sufferings and Jovial love for him becomes clear by Jupiter's explanation. Jupiter is a god of love as is God in Hebrews 12:6: *quem enim deligit Dominus, castigat* ("for whom the Lord loveth he chasteneth").[16] In this sense the theophany is an act of grace to Posthumus.

In *Cymbeline* the theme of fortune and providence is interlocked with that of appearance and reality which is another major theme of the play as well as other last plays. Until Jupiter confirms the rule of providence, the characters of the play appear to be under the rule of fortune which is destructive, malignant, and purposeless. However, this is only seeming not truth. Fortune blinds the characters from seeing reality. Fortune shows appearance and providence reveals reality. In this sense Fortune deceives the characters. Fortune as the trickster is in sharp contrast with providence as the revealer.

The idea of Fortune the trickster culminates in Act III and IV. In these acts the destructive action evolving around Imogen, Posthumus, and Cloten gets entangled and intensified. Pisanio explains to Imogen that her fortune is inscrutable at this moment. Moreover, he advises her to conceal her identity to avoid possible dangers which she might face if she did not do so: "Now if you could wear a mind / Dark as your fortune is, and disguise / That which, t'appear itself, must not yet be / But by self-danger" (III.iv 144-47). The word "dark" symbolizes both Imogen's pathetic situation and unintelligible operation of fortune. Pisanio tells Imogen to assume the costume of man to hide her reality. To show one's reality results in evoking danger. Pisanio knows how to survive in the unfathomable exercise of fortune.

Jupiter's descent resolves the inexplicably entwined

questions of appearance and reality / fortune and providence. Providence is both just and merciful. It exerts its final and decisive influence on human beings who seem to be in the control of fortune. Moreover providence clears entangled question of seeming and truth / appearance and reality.

In *Cymbeline* Shakespeare skillfully presents multifaceted levels of meanings through emblematic and emblem scenes whose understanding is crucial in grasping the whole thematic picture of the play. The thematically pivotal functions of emblems in the play are performed by the dynamic interrelationship between the visual and the verbal. This mature workmanship of Shakespeare in providing allegory-laden emblems is more manifest in *The Winter's Tale* which I will discuss in the next chapter.

Notes

1. Cesare Ripa, *Iconologia*, p. 84.
2. All references in this text to Peacham are to Henry Peacham, *Minerva Britanna, or a Garden of Heroical Devices*, 1612 (Leeds, England: The Scolar Press, 1966).
3. Douglas Peterson, *Time, Tide, and Tempest*, p. 128.
4. John Doebler, *Shakespeare's Speaking Pictures: Studies in Iconic Imagery* (Albuquerque, N. M.: U of New Mexico P, 1974), p. 138.
5. George Sandys, *Ovid's Metamorphosis Englished, Mythologized, and Represented in Figures*, ed., Karl K. Hulley and Stanley T. Vandersall (Lincoln: U of Nebraska P, 1970), p.403.
6. George Sandys, *Ovid's Metamorphosis*, p. 424.
7. Peter Daly, et al. eds., *Emblems in Translation*, Vol. 2 *of Andreas Alciatus* (Toronto: U of Toronto P, 1985), p. 98.
8. All references to Combe in this text are to Thomas Combe, *The Theater of Fine Devices*, 1614, ed. John Doebler (San Marino: The Huntington Library, 1983).
9. Jean Seznec, *The Survival of the Pagan Gods*, Trans. Barbara F. Sessions, Bollingen Series 38 (New York: Pantheon, 1953), p. 120.

10. Peterson, *Time, Tide, and Tempest*, p. 137.

11. Adolf Katzenellenbogen, *Allegories of the Virtues and Vices in Medieval Art: From Early Christian Times to the Thirteenth Century* (New York: Norton, 1964), p. 63.

12. Modern edition of the work is *The Rare Trimuph of Love and Fortune*, ed. John Isaac Owen (New York: Garland Publishing, 1979).

13. All quotations from Spenser are from *Spenser: Poetical Works*, ed. J. C. Smith and E. de Selincourt (Oxford: Oxford UP, 1912).

14. Quoted in *The Survival of the Pagan Gods*, p. 39 note 72.

15. Wilson Knight, *The Crown of Life* (London: Methuen, 1965), p. 201.

16. The Latin phrase is taken from *Novum Testamentum Latine* (Stuttgart: Deutsche Bibelgesellschaft, 1906).

CHAPTER 4

The Winter's Tale

An overview of *The Winter's Tale* leads to the conclusion that the play contains emblem and emblematic scenes whose structural and thematic roles are pivotal in understanding the play. Father Time and the sheep-shearing feast operate as emblem scenes and the bear and the statue scenes as emblematic ones. These emblem and emblematic scenes are integrated in the play to call our attention to some important aesthetic and ethical questions concerning Time the Destroyer and the Revealer, lust and chastity, fate and providence, and art and nature.

The iconographic image of Father Time is evidently seen in his attributes—"wings" and "glass." As has been already discussed in detail in *Pericles*, in Renaissance iconography Father Time is often portrayed as an old, winged man who holds a scythe, a sickle, or an hourglass in his hand. The wings, which are usually four in number, represent four seasons and the scythe, sickle, and hourglass symbolize the devastating and destructive power of time. The image of Father Time as the Destroyer is suggested in the chorus "it is in my power / To o'erthrow law and in one self-born hour / To plant and o'erwhelm the custom" (IV.i 7-9). Here the figure stresses his power to abolish and to establish human institutions. Obviously what the figure means by his "power" is natural decay or death. Besides the Destroyer, the figure has another image—the Revealer.

The image of Time as the Revealer is closely connected with the motif of *Veritas Filia Temporis* which predominated in Classical and Renaissance iconography and emblems. In the *Innocence* tapestry (*L'Innocentia del Bronzino*; Plate 10) in the Galleria degli Uffizi at Florence and in the famous *Allegory* in the London Gallery (Plate 5), Father Time is shown rescuing innocence, unmasking falsehood, and thus manifesting truth. In other words Father Time has the insight to detect falsehood and the power to reveal truth and to protect innocence. Whitney's emblem 4 (Plate 11) deals with this motif under the motto of *Veritas filia temporis*:

> THREE furies fell, which turne the worlde to ruthe,
> Both Enuie, Strife, and Slaunder, heare appeare,
> In dungeon darke they longe inclosed truthe,
> But Time at lengthe, did loose his daughter deare,
> And setts alofte, that sacred ladie brighte.
> Whoe things longe hidd, reueales, and brings to lighte.
> Though strife make fier, though Enuie eate hir harte,
> The innocent though Slaunder rente, and spoile:
> Yet Time will comme, and take this ladies parte,
> And breake her bandes, and bring her foes to foile.
> Dispaire not then, though truthe be hidden ofte,
> Bycause at lengthe, shee shall bee sett alofte.

Whitney explores the relationship between time, truth, and falsehood. Time rescues truth imprisoned in a dungeon by breaking the power of envy, strife, and slander. Like the artists of *Allegory* and *Innocence*, Whitney illuminates Time the Revealer. The above-mentioned iconography and emblem suggest the idea that Time is the final victor and ultimate resolver. In the speech of Time as chorus the idea of Time the Revealer is expressed as follows: "I, that please some, try all both joy and terror / Of good and bad, that makes and unfolds error, / Now take upon me, in the name of Time / To use my wings" (1-3). In spite of the syntactic ambiguity,[1] the quotation relates the revealing function of Time. Time judges between terror and joy, good and evil. Time uncovers truth and "unfolds" falsehood by testing. Time verifies and confirms through its test. Time as the tester shows us or leads us to the final outcome of events. It is doubtless that through the emblem scene of Father Time the playwright intends to deliver the moral and ethical imports of the figure—the Destroyer and the Revealer.

The moral and ethical implications of Father Time provide the framework for the understanding of the themes and structure of the play. The whole play hinges on the two aspects of Father Time. The first part of the play is largely devoted to the explication of the destructive power of Time and the second part mostly to the demonstration of the revelatory function of the figure. In this sense Time gives unity and coherence to the themes and structure of the play. The appearance of the figure in IV.i, which divides the first and second part, embodies the moral and ethical significance of the figure. The playwright visually presents the figure to the audience in order to underline its importance.

The destructive power of Time centers on the story of Leontes, who through his brutal jealousy brings about the disaster of the loss of his family. Although this disaster is not caused by Time's natural decay or death, it can still be explained in terms of time, especially the past. Destructive Time is revealed in Leontes's remembrance of the past. This past does not exist outside the king of Sicilia as an objective and neutral entity but remains as an affective and subjective entity operating in his consciousness. Leontes suddenly falls victim to jealousy when he is reminded of what Hermione promised three months after his wooing:

Why, that was when
Three crabbed months had soured themselves to death
Ere I could make thee open thy white hand
And clap thyself my love. Then didst thou utter
'I am yours forever.' (I.ii 101-5).

It took three months for him to win Hermione's love. At the recollection of the moment of his courting the distinction for him between the past and the present disappears. As a result he fails to differentiate what had happened between himself and Hermione from what is happening between Polixenes and her. For Leontes, the two events overlap and his past experience mirrors the present and the present echoes the past. Leontes views the friendship between his friend and his wife, influenced by his past desire for his wife.

His eruption of jealousy in I.ii is partly attributable to his free association of the present with the past. He seems to feel the passionate and amorous moment he enjoyed with Hermione when he watches Hermione give her hand to Polixenes:

[gives her hand to Polixenes and they walk apart]
Leontes[aside] Too hot, too hot!
  To mingle friendship far is mingling bloods.
  I have tremor cordis on me. My heart dances,
  But nor for joy, not joy. This entertainment
  May a free face put on, derive a liberty
  From heartiness, from bounty, fertile bosom,
  And well become the agent. ' T may I grant.
  But to be paddling palms and pinching fingers,
  As now they are, and making practiced smiles
  As in a looking-glass, and then to sigh, as ' were
  The mort o'th'deer. . . . (108-18)

Leontes's erotic phrases, "entertainment," "paddling palms," and "practiced smiles" disclose that he is recollecting his earlier desire for Hermione. As Douglas Peterson observes in *Time, Tide and Tempest*,[2] Leontes's remembrance of the past is at least an immediate cause of his jealousy which destroys his life. His past experience of desire for Hermione leaves the inerasable impression that women are "devils" (I.i 80) tempting men, and that Hermione is tempting Polixenes as she had tempted him. The first part of the play highlights Time the Destroyer in relation to the past whereas the second part the Time the Revealer in relation to the future.

Time the Revealer unmasks the falsehood of Leontes and discovers the truth and innocence of Hermione and Perdita. The death of Mamillus, the son of Leontes and Hermione, drives the hero to realize that he falsely convicted his wife of adultery. Time has exposed the evils of Leontes during the period of "twenty-three days" after the eruption of his jealousy. However it is not until the second part that Time fully vindicates innocence and upholds truth. Both the resurrection of Hermione and growth of Perdita bears out that truth and innocence defeat falsehood and evil. The last two scenes of the play, where the reunions and the resurrection are staged, are emblematically equivalent to the moment of Time's unveiling truth and embracing innocence as in the *Allegory* painting and the *Innocence* tapestry. An examination of *The Winter's Tale* convinces us of the fact that the emblem scene of Father Time is the framework on which the whole play is constructed. The thematic and structural importances of emblems in *The Winter's Tale* is again demonstrated by the sheep-shearing scene.

The whole scene of the sheep-shearing feast is to be interpreted as a theater emblem because of its morality and allegory. On a surface level the scene describes the sheep-shearing feast which was usually held in late June, though that in the play is much later, as Perdita suggests: "Sir the year is growing ancient, / Not yet on summer's death nor on the birth / Of trembling winter" (IV.iv 79-91). At this feast people enjoyed exchanging flowers, dancing to the tunes of bagpipes, and eating. However, the sheep-shearing feast in the play is not a typical one. Shakespeare modifies it, so that it is almost indistinguishable from other feasts such as the May game, or the feast of "Whitsun." One of the features of the May game is crowning Flora, the goddess of flowers. Spenser sings the ceremony of Flora in the May eclogue of *Shepheardes Calendar* (1579):

> I sawe a shole of shepheardes outgoe,
> With singing, and shouting, and iolly chere:
> Before them yode a lusty Tabrere,
> That to the many a Horne pype played,
> Whereto they daunceen eche one with his mayd.
> To see those folkes make such iouysance,
> Made my heart after the pype to daunce.
> Tho to the greene Wood they speeden hem all,
> To fetches home May with their musicall:
> And home they bringen in a royall throne,
> Crowned as king: and his Queene attone
> Was Lady Flora, on whom did attend
> A fayre flocke of Faeries, and a fresh bend
> Of louely Nymphs. (20-33)

In the May game shepherds go to forests, dancing with their partners and choose the King and the Queen, or Lady Flora. The sheep-shearing feast shares with the May game such features as crowning Lady Flora. The sheep-shearing feast hints at the ceremony of Flora-crowning: "These your unusual weeds to each part of you / Do give a life—not shepherdess, but Flora / Peering in April's front" (IV.iv 1-3). Florizel's mention of Flora adds another dimension of meanings to the feast. The playwright deliberately blends the features of the sheep-shearing feast and the May game for the purpose of imposing multilayered meanings on the scene.

Panofsky's comment on Giovanni Rost's *Flora* tapestry woven based on the cartoon drawn by Angelo Bronzino

(Plate 12) offers an insight into the allegorical meanings of the scene by underlining the similarity between the artist's work and the feast scene in the play.[3] In the tapestry, which should be called *"Primavera"* or "Spring," not *"Flora,"* a female figure dispenses flowers, hovering in the air with a ram, a bull, and the twins which stand for March, April, and May respectively. He points out that Primavera can be also identified as Venus.

Like Primavera Perdita dispenses flowers:

> You're welcome, sir.
> Give me those flowers there, Dorcas. Reverend sirs,
> For you there's rosemary and rue; these keep
> Seeming and savor all the winter long.
> Grace and remembrance be to you both,
> And welcome to our shearing! (IV.iv 72-77)

It is noteworthy that Perdita compares the ages of human life to four seasons. Spring is analogous to youth and winter to age. According to Panofsky the *Primavera* tapestry was originally designed to be one of four tapestries which represent the four seasons. The four seasons are closely related to four ages of human life as well as the four humors. In short, *Primavera* has multiple layers of meanings as Panofsky remarks: "Bronzino's *Primavera* implies, automatically, the notions of youth, air, and the sanguine temperament with all their secondary implications of gaiety and love."[4] Likewise the sheep-shearing scene does not literally describe a feast but conveys the moral meaning of lust and chastity and mythological one of resurrection and recovery.

A glance at Botticelli's *Primavera* (Plate 13) furthers our understanding of these meanings in the sheep-shearing feast. Unlike Rost's *Primavera* tapestry, Botticelli's painting features nine figures—Venus and her train, Flora, Mercury,

Cupid, the three Graces, and two other female figures. There is controversy about the identification of the two female figures. The three Graces dance while Cupid shoots an arrow in the air. It is beyond the scope of my study to discuss in detail the symbolic meanings of the painting.[5] Botticelli's vision of divinities remains enigmatic in spite of art historians' efforts to discover them fully. However we can identify at least two levels of meanings, if not all. One of them is mythological abstractions. As Jean Seznec remarks: "The great enigmas of Nature, of Death and Resurrection, seem to hover about these dreamlike forms of Youth, Love, and Beauty, phantoms from an ideal Olympus."[6]

The other is moral allegory. With regard to the moral allegory it is important to notice that the iconography is believed to be based on *The Judgment of Paris*.[7] According to Gombrich, the iconography of *The Judgment of Paris* "was traditionally read in the light of moral allegory. It rivalled the story of Hercules as an example of the moral choice before man . . . . the scene signifies the human choice between the three forms of life, contemplative, active, and voluptuous."[8]

Whitney's emblem 83 (Plate 14), whose motto is *Iudicium Parides*, proves that the motif of the judgment of Paris was introduced to Renaissance English culture:

To PARIS, here the Goddesses doe pleade:
With kingdomes large, did Ivno make her sute,
And PALLAS nexte, with wisedome him assaide,
But VENVS faire, did winne the goulden fruite.
    No princelie giftes, nor wisedome he did wey,
    For Bewtie, did comaunde him to obey.

The worldlie man, whose sighte is alwaies dimme,
Whose fancie fonde eache pleasure doth entice,
The shadowes, are like substance vnto him,
And toyes more deare, them thinges of greatest price:
    But yet the wise this iudgement rashe deride,
    And sentence giue on prudent PALLAS side.

Whitney moralizes the virtue of prudence Pallas exercises. It is not prudential to lead a voluptuous life, directed by "fancie fonde," as is attested by Paris. He condemns the voluptuous life which is opposed to the active or contemplative life.

The foregoing discussion lays the groundwork for probing into the multiple meanings of the feast scene of *The Winter's Tale*. In spite of the differences between Botticelli's *Primavera* iconography and the sheep-shearing feast, there are some striking affinities between them. The couple of Florizel and Perdita roughly parallels the figures of Mercury and Venus or Paris and Venus, and the shepherdesses the Graces. Moreover, the shepherdesses perform a dance as the Graces do.

In terms of mythological allegory the sheep-shearing scene deals with recovery and resurrection. While the first part of the play evolves around death and exile, the second part centers on restoration and regeneration. The sheep-shearing feast forms the background where this healing process happens. In the restorative process Perdita and Florizel play an important role. Their union in marriage implies the beginning of a new generation which is not influenced by the past disasters. In this sense Perdita can be said to represent allegorically "great creating nature" (IV.iv 88) as her dressing up as *Flora* or *Primavera* signifies. She is no more a shepherdess but the goddess of spring, who revives the world from the death of winter. Perdita's dispensing flowers means more than a mere part of the ceremony of the feast. It characterizes the scene where this revival occurs. In other words the feast scene does not necessarily refer to a specific and particular world of Bohemia but rather connotes a pastoral world of recovery and restoration. It is of no question that the playwright intends to contrast the pastoral scene of the second part with the disastrous story of the first part. However we need to be cautious because the pastoral

world of the sheep-shearing feast is a far cry from that of
Elysium or Arcadia. It is the world in which the bear
threatens men and Autolycus cheats them of their money.
Likewise, Perdita and Florizel are imperfect characters who
are taunted by lust rather than pure and innocent gods.
Shakespeare's vision of the pastoral world in sheep-shearing
feast in *The Winter's Tale* is not as ideal and perfect as that in
the masque scene in *The Tempest*.

In terms of moral allegory the sheep-shearing scene
elucidates the relationship between lust and chastity. This is
best demonstrated in Florizel and Perdita.[9] They are
tormented and disturbed by the conflict between sexual
desire and chaste life. Florizel's sexual desire for Perdita is
unveiled in the following speech:

> Apprehend
> Nothing but jollity. The gods themselves,
> Humbling their desires to love, have taken
> The shapes of beasts upon them. Jupiter
> Became a bull, and bellowed; the green Neptune
> A ram, and bleated; and the fire-robed god,
> Golden Apollo, a poor humble swain,
> As I seem now. Their transformations
> Were never for a piece of beauty rarer,
> Nor in a way so chaste, since my desires
> Run not before mine honor, nor my lusts
> Burn hotter than my faith. (24-35)

At first sight Florizel seems to claim his pure and innocent
love but he implicitly argues that lust is not so disgusting and
undesirable as Perdita might think. Even gods assume the
forms of beasts to satisfy their love. Conversely speaking,
Florizel has more reason than gods to pursue his lust. Even
though Florizel keeps his desires under control, they may
overpower him. Perdita has the insight to notice that his "true
blood," that is, his lust, lies beneath his audacious pretense
and outward appearance:

But that your youth,
And the true blood which peeps fairly through't,
Do plainly give you out an unstained shepherd,
With wisdom I might fear, my Doricles,
You wooed me the false way. (147-151).

Perdita is afraid that Florizel's "true blood" endangers their relationship. Florizel and Perdita do not succumb to the temptation of lust but keep it under their control. This brings them the final union of marriage.

Like Florizel Perdita experiences the impulse of lust. Her following speech exposes her hidden desire for lust:

I would I had some flowers o'th'spring that might
Become your time of day . . .
. . . . O Proserpina,
For the flowers now that, frighted, thou let'st fall
From Dis's wagon . . .
. . . . pale primroses,
That die unmarried, ere they can behold
Bright Phoebus in his strength—a malady
Most incident to maids. (IV.iv 113-25)

Perdita mentions the episode of the rape of Proserpina by Pluto. Along with other stories such as the Rape of Europa, Daphne and Apollo, Glaucera and Mercury, the episode of the rape of Proserpina shows "what happens when Chastity succumbs to Love."[10] She vaguely betrays her desire. Moreover she feels uneasy at seeing primroses, which signify greensickness, the malady of love. In conclusion the sheep-shearing scene as an emblem scene fuses multiple layers of meanings.

The three dances are integrated as significant visual emblems in the sheep-shearing feast—those of Perdita and Florizel, the shepherds and the shepherdesses, and the satyrs. Among the three dances the dance of the satyrs calls for our attention due to its allegorical meanings. The allegorical, pastoral, and festive features of the sheep-shearing feast, which are increasingly heightened by the first and the second dances, culminate in the last dance of the twelve satyrs. The servant gives a sketchy explanation of the dance:

> Master, there is three carters, three shepherds, three neatherds, three swineherds, that have made themselves all men of hair. They call themselves Saltiers, and they have a dance which the wenches say is a gallimaufry of gambols, because they are not in't; but they themselves are o'th mind, if it be not too rough for some that know little but bowling, it will please plentifully. (319-25)

According to the servant the performers of the satyrs' dance consist of twelve herdsmen who are divided into four groups, that is, "four threes of herdsmen." The twelve men appear in animal skins to disguise themselves as satyrs. In mythological traditions satyrs are represented by goat's head and cloven hoof. Another important thing in the servant's comment is that the satyrs' dance is "gallimaufry" and "rough." The dance is vigorous and does not follow certain rules. Based on the foregoing observations we can assume that the dance visually acts out the psychological transformation Florizel mentions in IV.iv 24-35.

That in the Renaissance a satyr is used as a symbol of animalistic lust leads us to the sexual symbolism in the dance. This symbolism is seen in Andreas Alciatus's emblems:

> Goat-footed Faunus, his temples wreathed with colewort (eruca), bears the fixed symbols of immoderate (immodicus) love (Venus). The colewort is lust-provoking (salax), and the goat is the symbol of lust (libido); and satyrs (satyrus) are always wont to love (amo) nymphs (nympha). (Emblem 72)

> The people worship (colo) Pan, that is to say, the nature (natura) of things,

a man half-goat, and a god (deus) half man.
He is a man (vir) to his loins, because virtue (virtus) implanted in us,
rising in the heart (cor), has its seat in the lofty citadel of the head (vertex)
Below the loins he is a goat (caper), because nature through the ages propagates (propago) us through intercourse (concubitus), like birds (volucris), scaly creatures, brutes and beasts (fera).
Because this is common to all living creatures, the goat is the symbol of lewdness (luxuria), and bears the clear marks of Venus.
Some attribute wisdom (sophia) to the heart, others to the brain (cerebrum)
Moderation (mondus), and not reason (ratio) restrains the lower faculties. (Emblem 98)

Satyrs figure forth lust in opposition to reason. Alciatus instructs us, however, to reconcile lust and reason instead of restraining the former with the latter. In the sheep- shearing scene the satyrs' dance visualizes the lust of the participants of the feast. The participants undergo psychological transformations caused by their release of sexual repressions in the festive atmosphere. Using C. L. Barber's expression, they show a pattern of "release to clarification."[11] They are released from emotional pressures arising from psychological factors such as sexual desires. Their release of sexual desires and psychological transformation are not necessarily monstrous and dangerous, rather it is natural. Sexual desires are to be controlled rather than repressed.

The bear scene in III.iii and the statue scene in V.iii are emblematic in that their immediate sources are not ascertained but they show the features of emblems such as tableau-likeness, morality, and allegory. Through the emblematic scenes Shakespeare also addresses moral and philosophical questions. The bear scene treats the destructive power of fate and the statue scene deals with the question of art and nature.

In the Renaissance the bear has two associations: a bear in a bear-baiting and a bear in the wilderness. A bear in a bear-baiting is trained to amuse the audience with its clumsy and slow movements. However, as with other ferocious animals such as tigers and lions, a wild bear produces a different association than a tamed bear. Antigonus implies a wild bear when he hears the animal cry: "a savage clamor" (III.iii 55). A wild bear is symbolic of natural savagery or wildness in the Renaissance literature.

To articulate the symbolism of the bear, two literary sources are especially useful: *The Faerie Queene* and *Mucedorous*. *Mucedorous*, which was one of the most popular plays in the Renaissance England, features a bear scene which resembles that in *The Winter's Tale*: "Enter Segasto running and Amadine after him, being pursued with a bear" (S.D. Scene iii). In the scene the bear poses a threat to the peaceful forest of Aragon. Thus the presence of this bear does not confer so much comicality as tragicality on the scene. In the Induction of *Mucedorous*, Comedy apostrophizes Envy:

> Thou, bloody, envious disdainer of men's joys,
> Whose name is fraught with bloody strategems,
> Delights in nothing but in spoil and death,
> Where thou mayst trample in their lukewarm blood,
> And grasp their hearts within thy cursèd paws. (41-45)[12]

Comedy uses an animal image in describing Envy ("within thy cursed paws") and the bear, likewise, is a symbol of destructive power. The bear in *Mucedorous* is not a comic device but a serious symbol. The bear is the agent of "death and spoil." Even though, according to Mouse, the bear seems to be impersonated by actor, the ferocity and savagery of the bear is not mitigated at all:

Mouse. Oh, horrible, terrible! Was ever poor gentlemen so scared
out of his even senses? A bear? Nay, sure it cannot be a bear, but
some devil in a bear's doublet for a bear could never have had that
agility to have frighted me. (ii.1-5)

Mouse's surprise evinces that the bear is a ferocious animal
even though it is enacted by an actor. Along with Bremo in
the forest, who signifies brutish naturalness without reason,
the bear adds a tragic element to the play.

A glance at *The Faerie Queene*, Book VI hints that it may
have influenced *The Winter's Tale*. The legend of S. Calidore
or courtesy, lends analogies with the play. In Canto IV
Calepine, a knight, rescues a baby from the mouth of a bear.
The poet's portrayal is powerful in portraying the cruelty and
ferociousness of the bear:

There him befell, vnlooked for before,
An hard aduenture with vnhappie end,
A cruell Beare, the which an intant bore
Betwixt his bloodie jawes, besprinckled all with gore. (17. 6-9)

Some lines later the poet gives another terrifying image of
the animal:

Wherewith the beast enrag'd to loose his pray,
Vpon him turned, and with greedie force
And furie, to be crossed in his way,
Gaping full wyde, did thinke without remorse
To be aueng'd on him, and to deuoure his corse. (20. 5-9)

Spenser is more concerned about the depiction of the
carnivorousness of the animal than is the anonymous
playwright of *Mucedorous*. In the poem the animal is more
dangerous and destructive than it is in the play. The bear
scenes in the poem and the play alike vividly transmit the
natural savagery and wildness in forests. However the beast
is beaten down by Calepine, who stands for courtesy and

Mucedorous, who connotes gentleness. In spite of its savage power the bear is not invincible. The poet and the anonymous playwright apparently share the idea that courtesy and gentleness can overpower natural violence which is sudden, malevolent, and purposeless.

Shakespeare inherits the tradition of the bear as a symbol of natural savagery and wildness, but he shapes his own dramatic symbol by modifying that tradition. The playwright emphasizes the animal's ferociousness to the extent that it seems invincible. To the audience of *The Winter's Tale* the carnivorous bear, which tears Antigonus, is threatening and deadly. The audience might be scared by the bear as Antigonus is. There seems to be no way to escape the beast. The bear as the symbol of unavoidable destructive power is explicitly buttressed by Andrew Gurr's review of a performance of the play:

> The 1982 Stratford production achieved this adroitly for both the naive and the knowing in the audience . . . . But when Antigonus quavered in the storm in III.iii, suddenly the backdrop was lit up with the image of a towering monster, twenty feet high, with raised claws and glaring eyes and fangs. The innocent and the knowing were equally shaken by the sight.[13]

The fact that the tempest accompanies the bear scene reinforces the symbolism of the bear's invincibility. Obviously the juxtaposition of the bear and the tempest scene is not coincidental but deliberate. As in *Pericles*, Act III Scene iii of *The Winter's Tale* delivers the uncontrollable power of fate in human beings who voyage in the sea of the world and who walk in the forest of the world. The clown's narration of the storm scene confirms that the two scenes are skillfully juxtaposed by their interlinking parallels:

> I would you did but see how it chafes, how it rages, how it takes up the shore. But that's not to the point. O, the most piteous cry of

the poor souls! Sometimes to see 'em, and not to see 'em. Now the ship boring the moon with her main-mast, and anon swallowed with yest and forth, as you'd thrust cork into a hogshed. And then for the land-service—to see how the bear tore out his shoulder-bone, how he cried to me for help and said his name was Antigonus, a nobleman. But to make an end of the ship—to see how the sea flapdragoned it. But, first, how the poor souls roared, and the sea mocked them, and how the poor gentleman roared and the bear mocked him, both roaring louder than the sea or weather. (84-97)

Both the tempest and the bear "swallow" and "rage." The clown takes note of the fact that the tempest and the bear alike destroy human lives. Thus the bear carries a similar emblematic meaning as the tempest. As human beings are like ships tossed on a sea, they are like Antigonus who is helplessly torn by the animal. Both the tempest and the bear are emblems of human fate which are characterized by irrationality, malevolence, and chance. In addition, the purposeless, destructive, and merciless fate will be intensified not only by visual but also auditory devices in case the sound effects of the storm and the bear cry are performed on the stage. The playwright is masterful in producing a total effect by combining visual and auditory as well as verbal devices. In performances the emotional impetus of the images would be overwhelming because of their fusing of action, speech, and sound effects.

Like the bear scene the statue scene is emblematic. The statue scene does not merely deal with the fantastic resurrection of Hermione but offers a deeper meaning. Moreover, the scene is static. The emblematic statue scene poses an aesthetic question, that is, a question about the relationship between art and nature. According to Edward William Tayler, in the Renaissance the division of art and nature functions as a framework to interpret almost everything such as cosmetics, gardening, and literature.[14] In other words, Renaissance people viewed the world based on the dichotomy of the artificial and the natural. For instance, in the sheep-shearing scene Polixenes and Perdita talk about subjects such as gardening, "painting," or cosmetics, and marriage. However, the statue scene voices particularly the question of dramatic representation and the superiority of, or at least the rivalry between dramatic art to other arts such as painting and sculpture.

It is necessary to examine the issue of the so-called paragon of arts in order for us to understand this aesthetic idea the playwright wills to communicate to the audience. Throughout the history of the arts there has been constant rivalry between them. Sculpture was regarded as superior to painting because of its mimetic representation, mainly its three-dimensional feature. Sculpture produces a better verisimilitude than painting. It is through this verisimilitude that sculpture contains essences of life in frozen or static moments. In sculpture a sculptor carves elusive and unstable essences of life in frozen forms. The demarcation between art and life or art and nature is tenuous in sculpture and for this reason the art is treated as superior to painting. Michelangelo was an ardent believer of the superiority of sculpture to painting. The Italian sculptor supports the idea of living sculpture as seen in his speech:

> This must be kept in mind that the closer you see paintings approach good sculpture, the better they will be; and the more sculptures will approach paintings, the worse you will hold them to be . . . . Let it be understood also that sculptures and reliefs, which perfect paintings resemble, are of course not only those of marble or bronze, but even more, *living* sculptures, like a handsome man, beautiful woman, a fine horse, and other similar things; and because the most true paintings are expressed with these, one sees then how wrong are those simpletons of whom the world is full, who would rather look at a green, a red, or some other high colors than at figures which show spirit and movement.[15] (italics mine)

The Italian maestro advocates the idea of living sculpture which captures life at given moment as exactly as possible. And since our life is three-dimensional, it follows that sculpture is superior to painting, which is two-dimensional.

The Pygmalion myth best champions sculpture as the paragon of art and the power of art over nature. In the myth the image of a woman carved by a sculptor is so identical to a living creature that he confuses the reality and the appearance. Interestingly in the Renaissance the myth of Pygmalion is so widespread as to appear frequently in literature, for instance, in John Marston's "The Metamorphosis of Pigmalion's Image."[16] For this reason it is quite possible that the playwright was more or less indebted to Ovid's description of Pygmalion as Arthur Fairchild mentions many times in *Shakespeare and the Arts of Design*: "In Shakespeare's adaptation of this story [Ovid], Pygmalion may be said to play a double part. As artist, he becomes Romano; as lover and husband, he becomes Leontes. Differences, such as the birth of the child . . . are insignificant; and there is a remarkable accord in details"[17]

The Ovidian story of a sculptor expounds sculpture' power to create nature by mimetically imitating it. A well-done imitation could be indistinguishable from nature. The Julio Romano passage convinces us of the mimetic power of art:

> No. The princess, hearing of her mother's statue, which is in the keeping of Paulina—a piece many years in doing and now newly performed by that rare Italian master, Julio Romano, who, had he himself eternity and could put breath into his work, would beguile Nature of her custom, so perfectly he is her ape. He so near to Hermione hath done Hermione that they say one would speak to her and stand in hope of answer. Thither with all greediness of affection are they gone, and there they intend to sup. (V.ii 89-98)

The sculptors demonstrate their masterful skill in reproducing nature as it is as an ape mimics human behavior.

It appears that with their masterly touch they breathed life into cold stone.

The impact of apish imitation on the beholder is exemplified by Leontes. He is amazed by the life-likeness of Hermione conceived to be a statue. He is impressed by the veins and wrinkles the living statue has. He can not distinguish between art and nature: "Masterly done / The very life seems warm upon her lip" (V.iii 65-66). The mimetic power of the statue makes him believe that it is alive and thus arouses his desire to kiss it. The statue with the veins and wrinkles is no more an imitation but seems life itself. The masterful workmanship of Julio Romano counterfeits nature so perfectly that the statue takes on the naturalness of life. However there is another concept of art. Art does not merely imitate but creates nature. Art invents, transforms, and modifies nature. An artist is a creator, not just an imitator. In the emblematic statue scene the playwright also calls our attention to the creative aspect of art as opposed to the imitative, especially with regard to the relationship between dramatic representation and sculptural imitation.

Like sculpture, drama imitates nature, as is seen in Hamlet's famous speech: "For anything so overdone is from the purpose of playing, whose end, both at the first and now, was and is, to hold, as'twere, the mirror up to nature" (III.ii 18-21). However, dramatic representation discerns itself from sculptural imitation. Drama does not apishly imitate nature. But in drama actors impersonate people other than themselves. This role-playing or acting is what makes drama. In a literal sense actors cannot be identical with the characters whose roles they play. There are wide gaps between the impersonators and the impersonated. Accordingly drama is regarded as inferior to sculpture in terms of verisimilitude. Nevertheless it is not just verisimilitude itself which bestows excellency on the arts. It is the beholder's imagination that is able to create anything out of nothing. Likewise, without the beholder's imagination, the statue would remain cold stone no matter how mimetically it is carved. Thus the question of how to activate and invigorate the audience's imagination is more important for the artist than how to imitate mimetically. In the emblematic statue scene it is Leontes's imagination rather than the mimetic imitation of the statue, which drives him to try to kiss it. This recalls Pygmalion's viewing his artistic work as perfect in his conceit as is described in John Marston's poem, "The Metamorphosis of Pigmalion's Image":

> Then view's her lips, no lips did seeme so faire
> In his *conceit*, through which he thinks doth file
> So sweet a breath, that doth perfume the ayre.
> Then next her dimpled chin he doth discry,
> And views, and *wonders*, and yet view's her still.
> "Loues eyes in viewing neuer haue their fill." (7; italics mine)

Like Richard II Leontes is born with an active imagination of a poet as is seen in I.ii. In the scene he had associated the friendly conversation of Polixenes and Hermione with his amorous relationship with her. As he uses his imagination in his destructive jealousy in the first part, he is required to employ the same faculty for a constructive purpose—the recovery of Hermione. I suggest that the "faith" Paulina asks him in the scene is fancy:

> It is required
> You do awake your faith. Then all stand still;
> Or those that think it is unlawful business
> I am about, let them depart. (94-97)

Paulina asks for the king's faith to believe that the statue is turning into a living woman. As the director of the scene, Paulina directs this speech not only to the on-stage audience but also to the off-stage audience.

Imagination is as integral in art as faith is in religion. Imagination is equated by Shakespeare with faith. In the emblematic statue scene the boundary between art and religion is indistinguishable. The resurrection of Hermione is an aesthetic as well as a religious event. Imagination and faith function in the same way. They bring forth impossibilities and produce wonders. The statue scene calls the audience's imagination or faith. The convergence of art and religion is lucidly noted by Howard Felperin:

> That art, as Paulina makes clear, requires that "You do awake your faith" (V.iii 94-95); the faith which now revives Hermione as its absence had previously "killed" her, but also the imaginative faith by which the entire scene works on the stage (no one who has seen the play well performed will doubt that it does work) by which we "credit [this] relation," in Pericles' phrase, "to points that seem impossible" even as we realize that there is no statue, that the art itself is nature, and that all can be rationally explained.[18]

Here Felperin's central idea is "imaginative faith." Both the audience's perception and the playwright's dramatic representation depend on an imaginative faith. To put it other way, the playwright and the audience cannot communicate with each other without this imaginative faith. It is imaginative faith that makes it possible for the playwright to stage the resurrection scene and for the audience to react to it with the same sense of wonder as Leontes. The impossible event of the resurrection can be enacted before the audience who watches it with imaginative faith.

In the statue scene Shakespeare challenges Romano's skill to apishly imitate. The playwright professes his power to provoke the audience's imaginative faith. For him drama is no more inferior to sculpture than he is to Romano. Paulina, like Prospero, performs more wonderful magic than other artists such as sculptors and painters. Dramatists are magicians who can perform the wonders of resurrections and transformations: "If this be magic, let it be an art / Lawful as eating" (111-12). For the playwright drama is the paragon of arts. To those watch the play with imaginative faith, it becomes magic and to those who do not, it is merely "like an old tale."

In *The Winter's Tale* the emblem scenes of Father Time and the sheep-shearing feast and the emblematic bear and statue scenes raise significant philosophical and moral as well as aesthetic questions which have great bearing on the themes and the structure of the play. The thematic and structural importances of emblem and emblematic scenes are also true of *The Tempest* which I will discuss in the next chapter.

Notes

1. For this, see Jay Ludwig, "Shakespearean Decorum: An Essay on *The Winter's Tale*," *Style* 8:2 (1974): 379-81.
2. Douglas Peterson, pp. 157-160.
3. Panofsky, *Studies in Iconology*, pp. 85-86.
4. Panofsky, p.86.
5. For the past scholarship on the interpretation of the painting, see E. H. Gombrich, *Symbolic Images: Studies in the Art of the Renaissance* (London: Phaidon, 1972), pp.31-64.
6. Jean Seznec, *The Survival of the Pagan Gods*, p.113.
7. E. H. Gombrich, *Symbolic Images*, P.46.
8. E. H. Gombrich, *Symbolic Images*, p.54.
9. Douglas Peterson, *Time, Tide, and Tempest*, pp. 171-73.
10. Jean Seznec, *The Survival of the Pagan Gods*, p.109.
11. C. L. Barber, *Shakespeare's Festive Comedy*, p.4.
12. The quotation is taken from Russell Fraser and Norman Rabkin, ed., *Drama of the English Renaissance*, 2 vols. (New York: Macmillan, 1976).

13. Andrew Gurr, "The Bear, The Statue, and Hysteria in *The Winter's Tale,"* *Shakespeare Quarterly* 34 (1983): 423 note 10.

14. Edward Tayler, *Nature and Art in Renaissance Literature* (New York: Columbia UP, 1964), pp. 11-37.

15. Quoted in Robert Clements, *Michelangelo's Theory of Art* (New York: Gramercy Publishing Company, 1961), pp.311-12.

16. The quotation is taken from John Marston, *The Poems of John Marston*, ed. Alexander Grosart (Manchester, 1879).

17. Arthur Fairchild, *Shakespeare and the Arts of Design*, U of Missouri Studies, 12. No. 1 (Columbia: U of Missouri P, 1937), P.73.

18. Howard Felperin, *Shakespearean Romance* (Princeton: Princeton UP, 1972), P.242.

CHAPTER 5

The Tempest

Shakespeare's craftsmanship in adapting emblems to plays reaches near perfection in *The Tempest*. It is true that *The Winter's Tale* also shows the playwright's ability to exploit emblems for dramatic purposes. However, his skill to erect emblems on the stage is even more adroit and creative in *The Tempest* than in *The Winter's Tale*. Moreover, in the play he fully experiments with the various kinds of theater emblems—auditory, visual, and the combination of the two—by using actors' speeches, gestures, and sound effects.

The storm scene in I.i and the harpy scene in III.iii belong to emblem scenes, and Ariel's songs, "Come unto these yellow sands" and "Full fathom five thy father lies" in I.ii, the masque scene in IV.i, and the hunting scene in IV.i comprise emblematic scenes. Through the emblem scenes Shakespeare invites the audience to consider the relationship between fortitude and patience, and fate and providence. Through the emblematic scenes the playwright handles the questions of chastity and fertility, harmony and purgation, and passion and reason. It is worth noting that the emblem and emblematic scenes are performed by the characters in the play. Except for Ariel's songs, all of the emblem and emblematic scenes are presented by speech and action.

The Tempest begins with the storm scene. The emblem scene employs both actors' actions and speeches, which deliver the picture and the epigram of the emblem respectively. In the storm scene sound effects perform a vital role. The stage description in the beginning convinces us of the role of the sound effects: "A tempestuous noise of thunder and lightning heard." The appeal of the auditory effect is direct and immediate. The audience perceives that the play begins with the storm. The picture of the storm emblem is impressively represented by the auditory effect.

Like the storm scenes in *Pericles* and *The Winter's Tale*, that in *The Tempest* offers the whole and coherent picture of the relationship between patience and fortitude on the one hand, and that between fate and providence on the other hand. The theme of *fortitudo-patientia* is best shown in the boatswain. He has the courage to cope with the storm. However, his courage is far from audaciousness or recklessness like that of Antonio and Sebastian who defy nature and the gods. The boatswain's virtue provides Gonzalo with the hope for survival in the storm: "I have great comfort from this fellow: me thinks he hath no drowning mark upon him; his complexion is perfect gallows. Stand fast, good Fate, to his hanging! Make the rope of his destiny our cable, for our own doth little advantage" (I.i 26-30). The boatswain is so brave in the midst of the storm that he seems to be fated to die on land. If this is so, his fate holds good for himself as well as for others. Gonzalo holds on to "the rope of his destiny" for the hope of his survival.

The Tempest centers on the theme of *fortitudo-patientia* which I discussed in the Patience emblem in V.i of *Pericles*. Prospero is first and foremost a man of patience and fortitude. He does not fall into despair when he is banished by his brother Antonio but he demonstrates the remarkable courage to "bear up / Against what should ensue" (I.ii 156-57). In addition he is remarkable for his patience of waiting for twelve years until "By accident most strange, bountiful Fortune / (Now, my dear lady) hath mine enemies / Brought to this shore" (I.ii 178-80). He waits on divine will to recover his personal honor and to restore the political and moral disorder of Milan. Prospero's virtues of *fortitudo-patientia* act as a major agent of bringing about the happy ending in the play.

Ferdinand is another character who is marked by *fortitudo-patientia*. In I.ii he is accused of his treason by Prospero. Ferdinand defies Prospero in protest against Prospero's false accusation. This event parallels Pericles in the court of Simonides who charges the hero with the treason of seducing his daughter, Thaisa. Ferdinand's defiance of Prospero's false accusation proves him to be a man of fortitude. Moreover, Ferdinand's patience is tested when he is told to carry logs for Prospero: "And for your sake / Am I this patient logman" (III.i 57). However, he patiently endures the labor of carrying logs and this leads him to the marriage with Miranda. The *fortitudo-patientia* of both Prospero and Ferdinand stems from their hope. Prospero believes in "providence divine" (I.ii 160) and Ferdinand hopes for Miranda's love. Their hope sustains them with the virtues of endurance, perseverance, generosity, and patience, all of which belong to fortitude.

In the storm scene the question of *fortitudo-patientia* is infused with that of fate and providence. The characters appear to be fated to destruction. The "confused noise within" (S.D. 57) aurally conveys the groan of the characters under the power of fate: "Mercy on us!— / We split, we split!—Farewell, my wife and children!— / Farewell, brother!—We split, we split, we split!" (58-60). The repeated cries of "we split, we split" give expression to the harsh and ruthless rule of fate. As mariners' cry suggests, all seem to be lost: "All lost! To prayers, to prayers! All lost!" (I.i 47). Mariners resort to divine power in the situation where they are crushed by fate. Fate is too powerful to be handled by human power.

It is Gonzalo who pays attention to providential operation. He sees the possibility that providence may rescue himself from the storm:

> Now would I give a thousand furlongs of sea for an acre of barren ground—long heath, brown furze, anything. The wills above be done, but I would fain die a dry death. (60-63)

Gonzalo's entreatment of providence is suggested by the fact that the prayer is unmistakably penetrated by a Christian strain. He trusts his life to "the wills above." The phrase, "the wills above done," undoubtedly echoes the Lord's Prayer. Interestingly the beginning and the end of *The Tempest* are impregnated with Christian terms and concepts. Prospero's epilogue is also modeled on the Lord's Prayer: "Unless I be relieved by prayer, / Which pierces so that it assaults / Mercy itself and frees all faults" (16-18). Prospero depends on the Lord's Prayer in order to invoke the Holy Spirit who can mediate between himself and God and forgive sins.

The storm emblem in the beginning of *The Tempest* sheds light on the question of fate and providence in relation to *patientia-fortitudo*. In the ending of the play this question is given an answer that providence is in final and decisive control of human destiny. As in the other last plays, the purposeful, restorative, and benign operation of providence is in a stark contrast with the purposeless, malevolent, and destructive conduct of fate. Providence endows man with *fortitudo-patientia* and fate drives man to despair. The question of fate and providence is treated from another perspective, that is, divine mercy and justice, in the banquet scene in III.iii.

The banquet scene in III.iii marks another emblem scene which is performed by Ariel and his spirits under the direction of Prospero. The scene consists of three separate dumb shows. In the first dumb show several strange shapes bring in a banquet and dance around it, inviting the shipwrecked nobles to the feast. In the second dumb show Ariel appears as a harpy in thunder and the banquet vanishes. In the third dumb show Ariel as a harpy disappears in thunder and the strange shapes reappear and dance again. In the three dumb shows the banquet and the harpy symbolism draws our special attention.

The banquet scene does not operate as celebration of a feast. Rather it is designed to lead the three sinners—Alonso, Sebastian, and Antonio—to admit their sins and to repent as Ariel's speech on providence after the second dumb show signifies. In this light the banquet is symbolic as well as literal. The banquet is an allegorical representation of the sinner's sins, especially greed. After wandering in the island the sinners become hungry and their strong appetite is aroused by the banquet. As Comus tempts the lady to join his banquet by preparing the table "spread with all dainties," Ariel entices the sinners with the banquet table brought in by the strange shapes. In his iconographic study of Comus in Ben Jonson's *Pleasure Reconciled to Virtue*, Stephen Orgel argues that a banquet had been traditionally associated with the god of revelry.[1] In view of this a banquet is interpreted as an emblem of sensual appetite for food, liquor, and sex. A banquet as a symbol of sensual appetites is excellently expostulated in an emblem titled "Burghers at Revels" in an emblem book, *Viridarium Hieroglyphico-Morale . . .* (Frankfurt 1619) by Heinrich Assenheim. The emblem, whose motto is "Without Ceres and Bacchus, Venus grows cold," moralizes the virtue of temperance:

Aloga habent certas potandi animantia leges,
Ultra demensum bellua nulla bibit:
Nos homines autem recta ratione vigentes,
(Nos madidus Iacchus nocte dieque rigat.
(Unreasoning creatures have fixed laws of drinking.
No beast drinks intemperately.
We men, however, flourishing in right reason—
dripping Iacchus [Bacchus] moistens us night and day.)[2]

The German emblematist features the paradox that beasts
lacking reason shows temperance in drinking, whereas
rational man indulges in the activity intemperately. The icon
of the emblem pictures the burghers whose sensual pleasure
transforms them into pigs. Their doomed death is suggested
by the two death figures: one hosts the banquet and the other
enters through the window.

Henry Peacham includes Emblem 174 (Plate 15), which
has almost the same motto (*sine Cerere et Baccho*) and poem
as the German emblem, but a different picture:

SAY *Cytharaean* maid, why with thy sonne,
Both handes and feete thon warmest at the fire?
Who wont your selues, t'enkindle many a one,
With gentle flames, of kindly loues desire:
    I ghesse cause *BACCHVS* is not present heere,
With mirthfull wine, nor *CERES* with her cheere.
Where Temp'rance and Sobrietie do raigne,
There lustfull vice, and pleasure frozen are:
And vertue best, there liketh to remaine;
When often times th'effectes of daintie fare,
    And drunken healthes, are quarrelles and debate,
    Blaspheming, whoredome, oaths and deadlie hate.

According to Peacham, Venus and Cupid cannot exercise
their power to enkindle "loues desire" without the help of
Bacchus and Ceres who are often called the god and the
goddess of wine and bread in the Renaissance mythology.
Without the aid of Bacchus and Ceres Venus and Cupid

cannot hold a banquet where vices such as drunkenness and quarrels are committed. These vices are effected by "daintie fare," that is, delicious food. Like Assenheim Peacham voices the virtues of temperance and sobriety as opposed to the vice of sensual appetite. Peacham's emblem particularly highlights Stephano, Trinculo, and Caliban.

Assenheim and Peacham suggest two facts in regard to the understanding of the banquet scene in *The Tempest*. First the banquet scene concerns sensual pleasure and, second, the strange shapes in the scene may represent vices or sins. John Doebler goes further to identify the shapes with the Seven Deadly Sins:

> Shakespeare clearly wants us to interpret the banquet in *The Tempest* as an emblem of sin. In the original staging of the play, this dramatic purpose may even have been conveyed to the audience by hinting at the conventional stage appearance of the Seven Deadly Sins in the costuming and behavior of the "strange shapes" who bring in the banquet in, making it a procession like that of the Seven Deadly Sins in *Doctor Faustus*.[3]

Doebler claims that the banquet scene may be derived from the Banquet of Sin, which is a transformation of the Banquet of Sense seen in Assenheim. Doebler further contends that the Banquet of Sin has two sources: biblical and allegorical.[4] The story of the prodigal son in the New Testament offers a biblical source, and Spenser's allusion to the entertainment of the Red Cross Knight before the procession of the seven deadly sins supplies an allegorical source. Doebler also suggests that the strange shapes are possibly the Seven Deadly Sins. Given the fact that the Seven Deadly Sins are accompanied by respective beasts in the Renaissance pageantry, it is convincing that the strange shapes may refer to them. For instance, in The First Booke of *The Faerie Queene* (iv. 15) the Seven Deadly Sins—Idleness, Gluttony, Lechery, Avarice, Envie, Wrath, and Sloth—ride on respectively an ass, a swine, a goat, a camel, a wolf, a lion, and a wagon. Placing the banquet scene in *The Tempest* in the tradition of Banquet of Sin and interpreting the strange shapes as the pageant of the Seven Deadly Sins, the scene serves the moral purpose of teaching the three sinners the virtue of temperance and helping them to shun the vice of sensual appetite. The banquet mirrors their inner desire to run after sensual pleasures. Prospero's aside exposes their true reality: "Honest lord, / Thou hast said well; for some of you there present / Are worse than devils" (III.iii 34-35). In spite of their noble appearance their inner reality is bestial.

Shakespeare ascribes private immoral actions to sensual pleasures. Indulging in sensual pleasures leads man to commit vices and sins. For instance, sexual desire, which may be aroused by drunkenness, tempts the three drunkards— Caliban, Stephano, and Trinculo—to make an attempt to murder Prospero and rape Miranda. The three drunkards exemplify the effects of sensual life on their moral corruption. Likewise, the three sinners are likely to give in to the temptation of sensual appetite. The banquet is a device to refrain the sinners from sensual pleasures. The sinners are held back from sensual indulgence partly for the purpose of preventing them from moral corruption and partly for the purpose of safeguarding and preserving innocent people such as Miranda and Ferdinand.

The harpy scene in the second dumb show is closely connected with the banquet scene. Ariel appears as a harpy and claps wings on the table, which "vanishes with a quaint device." Even though there may be other interpretations concerning the relationship between the disappearance of the banquet and the harpy, it is strongly suggested that the harpy devoured it. Some lines after the stage description Prospero hints at this: "Bravely the figure of this harpy has thou / Performed, my Ariel; a grace it had, devouring" (83-84). The word, "devouring," implies that Ariel eats up the banquet as a beast of prey. In Milton's *Paradise Regained* the food-loaded table, which Satan spreads to tempt the Son of God, vanishes with the appearance of harpies: "Both Table and Provision vanish'd quite / With the sound of Harpies' wings and Talons heard" (II. 401-3). Milton also insinuates that harpies devoured the table.

It is not until we take a look at Virgil's *The Aeneid* that we come to fully grasp the symbolic meaning of the harpy scene. In the Third Book of the epic poem Virgil narrates the arrival of Aeneas and his men in the island of Strophades in the great Ionian sea which are "the home of horrible Celaeno / and all her sister Harpies since the time / that Phineus shut his house against them and, / in fear, they fled their former feasts" (278-81).[5] A few lines after this description Virgil explains the harpy symbolism: "No monster is more malevolent than these, no scourge / of gods or pestilence more savage ever rose from the Stygian waves" (281-84). Harpies stand for divine wrath or anger. Actually Celaeno calls itself the "eldest Fury" (*Furiarum maxima*).[6] According to Virgil harpies are created to punish Phineus, a legendary king of Salmydessus. George Sandys (1578-1644) gives a more comprehensive emblematic rendering of the harpy in the Seaventh Booke of his *Ovid's Metamorphosis*:

> *The Harpyes* are so named of Rapine: said to be virgins in that barren; because goods so gotten descend but seldome to posterity: to fly, in that swift in extorting: to be covered with plumes, for cloking their prey: and to have the talons of vultures, of griping, and fast-holding of their ill-got riches. These qualities are also caractered in their names, *Aello, Ocipetes, and Celeno* . . . . They are fained to be the daughters of *Neptune and Tellus*; of old esteemed the parents of prodigies and are called *Jupiters* dogges; that is, infernal Furies: here introduced to snatch the meat from *Phineus* table; because those were said . . . to be afflicted by the Furies, who covetously abstained from the use of their owne.[7]

The harpies, which are called by another name "Jupiters dogges," snatch away "ill-got riches" with their talons of vultures. They bring Jupiter's wrath on covetous people as "infernal Furies." In short they are the means of the punishment by the gods. As furies strike thunder in the face of Tantalus in Hades who is about to feed a banquet, the harpies torment the greedy Phineus.

In relation to the harpy as the emblem of divine retribution Doebler equates the harpy and Nemesis, who is described as the "winged vengeance" in III.vii 65 of *King Lear*[8] and supports his idea with some iconography on the goddess of justice (for the iconography see Plate 34 in Doebler). Nemesis is a female figure with wings, not a bird with a woman's face. Considering the fact that Ariel is a winged figure, the character is closer to the goddess than to a harpy like the one in *The Aeneid* which has a bird's body and a woman's face. We need to recollect the fact that in the Renaissance there were two kinds of harpies: a woman with wings and a bird with a woman's face. Whether Shakespeare means the former or the latter by the harpy, it is certain that he intends to convey the concept of divine wrath to the audience through the emblem

The moral meaning of the harpy emblem is clearly articulated in Ariel's speech following the scene:

I and my fellows
Are ministers of Fate.
. . . .
for which foul deed
The pow'rs, delaying, not forgetting, have
Incensed the seas and shores, yea, all the creatures,
. . . .
whose wraths to guard you from,
Which here, in this most desolate isle, else falls
Upon your heads, is nothing but heart's sorrow
And a clear life ensuing. (III.iii 60-82)

Prospero tries to plant the sense of destiny in Antonio in order to lead him to repentance. He introduces the Machiavellian to the idea that he cannot be absolved from the consequences of the crimes which he committed. His vices call for the divine wrath which hangs above him. Ariel and his fellows, who serve Prospero's purpose, act as "ministers of fate" to Antonio. Ariel clarifies that it is divinity (actually Prospero who impersonates deity) that raises the tempest and that the sinners stand the trial of their crimes. They are exonerated only when they live a repentant life ("clear life"). Here Ariel assumes the role of a ministering angel of Prospero. Ariel reminds Antonio of the presence of divinity which has ultimate control over humans and nature.

It is worth mentioning that the harpy emblem in *The Tempest* is sharply distinguished from that in *Pericles*. The harpy in *Pericles* (IV.iii 46) is an aural emblem of hypocrisy whereas that in *The Tempest* is a visual emblem of divine punishment. Moreover, the harpy emblem in *The Tempest* is a nexus which connects the question of fate and providence as well as that of divine mercy and justice on the other hand. Providence shows its justice by calling sinners such as Sebastian and Antonio to the trial. In addition it confirms its mercy by rescuing innocent Prospero and Miranda.

Ariel's two songs in I.ii are an auditory emblematic scene which enunciates the significant moral ideas of harmony and purgation. These ideas formulate another leading theme together with that of fate and providence, patience and fortitude, and passion and reason. The fact that this emblematic scene is exclusively made up of songs and sound effects draws our special attention. In the scene the audience is totally dependent on its auditory perception, since the emblematic scene consists of Ariel's two songs and the sound effects of the animal sounds and the bell. Besides this

Ariel is expected to be invisible. The playwright skillfully conveys the emblem scene only with auditory devices.

Ariel's first song opens up the world of the spirits which dance on the yellow sands beside the calm sea:

> Come unto these yellow sands,
>   And then take hands.
> Curtsied when you have and kissed,
>   The wild waves whist,
> Foot it featly here and there;
>   And, sweet spirits, the burden bear.
> *Burden, dispersedly.* Bowgh, wawgh!
>   The watchdogs bark.
> *Burden, dispersedly.* Bowgh, wawgh!(375-83)

The song portrays the dance of the spirits which take hands, curtsy, and kiss. The spirits' dance is accompanied by the burden, a kind of refrain, of the watchdogs. The world of the spirits is mysterious and supernatural. The spirits' dance on the yellow sands produces the emblematic image of harmony. Harmony is emblematically represented by the juxtaposition of the graceful movements of the spirits and the undulation of the waves. The supernatural fairies are in good harmony with the sea. Nature and the spiritual world correspond with each other. This vision of harmony is the ultimate goal the play aims to present. The picture of concord and peace between the spirits and the calm sea provides a stark contrast to that of the conflict and contention between the shipwrecked men and the surging sea in the beginning scene. In this light the dance of the spirits foreshadows that of the reapers and the nymph in the masque in III.iii.

The poetic vision of harmony in Ariel's song is undercut by the music and the sound effects. The fact that Ariel does not just recite the songs but sings them is worth noticing. In a sense the music exercises more immediate and stronger effects on the audience than the poem as is hinted by

Ferdinand's comment: "This music crept by me upon the waters, / Allaying both their fury and my passion / With its sweet air" (I.ii 392-94). Ferdinand responds to the tunes rather than to the verse of the song. Interestingly, after the harpy scene, Alonso declares that he is overwhelmed by the music of the waves rather than by the speech of Ariel: "and the thunder, / That deep and dreadful organ pipe, pronounced / The name of Prosper" (III.iii 97-99). The king is awe-stricken, especially by the burden of Prosper made by the thunder which is compared to an organ pipe.

The dogs and the cock convey significant meanings in Ariel's music. Ferdinand's speech on Ariel's music is a clue to investigating the aural symbolism of the sound effects. The prince of Naples confesses that he is cured of his deadly melancholy by the music as seen in the speech quoted above. What the prince mentions here is the therapeutic function of *musica instrumentalis*.

The notion of musical therapy is closely interlocked with the concept of harmony which has played a pivotal role in the development of the Western music. In his *The Untuning of the Sky* John Hollander defines the concept as "the ordering of simultaneously sounding musical tones."[9] This theory of harmony is the basis on which *musica humana* and *musica mundana* are constructed. The two musical theories claim that the constituents of the human soul generate different tones which create *musica humana* as the planets play *musica mundana*. The harmony of *musica humana* and *musica mundana* is achieved only when the constituents of the human soul and the universe are combined proportionately. The ancient philosophers explain the cosmological and psychological aspects of music by the theory of pitches and scales of instrumental or practical music. The music of the spheres and the human soul, which is imperceptible to the human ear, is materialized by the sounds of instrumental music. Therefore the harmonious instrumental music was believed to have a therapeutic effect on the hearer. The disproportionate jarrings of the human soul are restored by the harmonious tunes of instrumental music.

With regard to the question of how the concept of harmony illuminates the aural symbolism of the sound effects of Ariel's song, we need to pay attention to the fact that the noises of hounds and cocks can substitute for harmonious instrumental music. Like musical instruments the animals can make harmonious sounds. Accordingly the hound cries in I.ii take on a very different meaning from those in the hunting scene in IV.i. In I.ii the animal noise is an aural symbol of harmony and perfection whereas in IV.i it is that of destruction and death. In the former scene the animal sound is polyphony while in the latter it is cacophony.

The notion of harmonious sounds of hounds is not strange to an audience who is familiar with *A Midsummer Night's Dream*. In the episode of the hunting in IV.i of the play, Theseus boasts about his dogs, which bark more harmoniously than Hippolyta's:

> My hounds are bred out of Spartan kind:
> . . . .
> Crook-kneed, and dewlapped like Thessalian bulls;
> Slow in pursuit, but matched in mouth like bells,
> Each under each. A cry more tuneable
> Was ever halloed to nor cheered with horn
> In Crete, in Sparta, nor in Thessaly. (118-25)

In the play the hounds are accounted for as animals making such harmonious sounds as the bells do. Theseus remarks that the hound sounds are more harmonious than a horn. J. Dover Wilson cites a passage from Cervase Markham's pamphlet on *Countrey Contentments* (1611) which hints the possibility of arranging the hound sounds to form a three-part chorus of bass, counter-tenor, and mean:

If you would have your kennel for sweetness of cry, then you
must compound it of some large dogs that have deep solemn
mouths and are swift in spending, which must, as it were, bear the
bass in the consort, then a double number of roaring and loud
ringing mouths which must bear the counter-tenor, then some
hollow plain sweet mouths which must bear the mean or middle
part; and so with these three parts of music you shall make your
cry perfect.[10]

The playwright of *The Tempest* aims to produce
harmonious sounds of the dogs to convey image of harmony
aurally. This is also true of the cocks. The music of Ariel
consisting of the song and the sound effects is so tuneable as
to pacify the passion of Ferdinand and the tempestuous sea.
Ferdinand is one of an ideal audience which experiences
what the playwright wants it to do.

Ariel's second song describes the sea-change which
Alonso undergoes:

Full fathom five thy father lies;
    Of his bones are coral made;
Those are pearls that were his eyes;
    Nothing of him that doth fade
But doth suffer a sea-change
Into something rich and strange.
Sea nymphs hourly ring his knell:
Burden. Ding-dong.
Hark! Now I hear them—Ding-dong bell. (397-404)

The king of Naples's change is not just transformation but
transubstantiation in that his bones become coral and his eyes
pearls. He is in the process of being born into something
"rich and strange." In order to be improved morally , the king
needs to be purged of his sins. The song, therefore, does not
poetize a gross image of Alonso. Rather, it versifies the
process of his purgation in a metaphoric way.

The theme of purification also underlies the aural
symbolism of the bell sounds. As a funeral knell the bell

indicates the fact that the king's old self is buried in the deep sea and his new self emerges as a result of the sea change. Based on this observation the king's sea-change is viewed as an equivalent of baptism. The sea nymphs perform the ceremony of baptizing the sinner in a deep sea to make him a new creature. Like Ariel the nymphs are divine ministering angels which officiate a baptism ceremony for the salvation of the king.

The bell sound as the symbol of vice-free soul is attested in *A Book for Boys and Girls*, an emblem book without icons by John Bunyan. In Emblem XXIX, Bunyan moralizes the ringing of bells by employing the analogy of the instrument-organ:

> *Comparison*
> These bells are like the Powers of my soul;
> Their Clappers to the Passions of my mind.
> The Ropes by which my Bells are made to tole,
> Are promises (I by experience find.)
> My body is the Steeple, where they hang,
> My Graces they which do ring ev'ry Bell:
> Nor is there anything gives such a tang,
> When by these Ropes these Ringers ring them well.
> Let not my Bells these Ringers want, nor Ropes;
> Yea let them have room for to swing and sway:
> To toss themselves deny them not their Scopes.
> Lord! in my Steeple give them room to play.
> If they do tole, ring out, or chime all in,
> They drown the tempting tinckling Voice of Vice:
> Lord! when my Bells have gone, my Soul has bin
> As ' twere a tumbling in this Paradice!
> Or if these Ringers do the Changes ring,
> Upon my Bells, they do such Musick make,
> My Soul then (Lord) cannot but bounce and sing,
> So greatly her they with their Musick take.
> But Boys (my Lusts) into my Belfry go,
> And pull these Ropes, but no Musick make.
> They rather turn my Bells by what they do,
> Or by disorder make my Steeple shake.[11] (1-24)

Bunyan compares the body to the steeple, the ringer to Graces, and the ropes to divine promises. Divine graces make the ring of the bell in his soul when they hold on to the promises. He prays that he may keep the graces which make beautiful ring in his soul. When he lacks this bell sound produced by the graces, he is engulfed by "the tempting tinckling voice of vice." Lust and vice make disorder and cacophony in his soul. The bell sounds represent the state of the soul where graces rule his soul and neither "Lusts" nor "Vice" affect him. He feels that the two opposing powers contending with each other to dominate his soul. Caught in this dilemma, he asks God to exercise his full control over his soul so that it may produce the changes, that is, harmonious ringing of the different tones of the bells. Bunyan uses the bell as a symbol representing the virtuous and graceful state of soul.

Thomas Traherne (1637-1674) also employs the bell-purification metaphor. In Part II of his "Bells" the poet is concerned about how ore is tempered into the metal out of which the bell is made. Being refined by fire, baser ore is changed into purer metal:

From Clay, and Mire, and Dirt, my Soul,
From vile and common Ore,
Thou must ascend; taught by the Toll
In what fit place thou mayst adore:
Refin'd by fire, thou shalt a Bell
Of Prais becom, in Mettal pure;
In Purity thou must excell,
No Soil or Grit endure.
Refined by Lov,
Thou still *abov*
Like them must dwell, and other Souls allure . . . . [12]

Traherne sees the bell as the metaphor of purgation and purity. As baser ore is refined into pure metal, so the human soul ascends to heaven by purging itself of impurities. The phrase, "thou still abov," indicates the possibility of transcending this human world and reaching the heavenly state. Both Bunyan and Traherne shed light on the fact that the bell sounds are not earthly but heavenly in that they are related to the holiness and purity which transcend this world.

Bunyan's and Traherne's uses of the bell as the emblem of heavenly purity and innocence seem to be based on the emblem tradition of the Renaissance. In Emblem 15 Andreas Alciatus interprets the moral of the bell-sounding and the cock- crowing as follows:

> A crowing cock(gallus), because it signals the coming dawn,
> and recalls toiling hands to a new day's work;
> a bronze bell, because it recalls wakeful(vigil) minds(mens) to
>   heavenly things,
> are represented on the holy(sacer) towers(turris)
> And what is more, as guardian(custos) there is a lion(leo), because
>   it sleeps(dormio) with open eyes(oculus)
> and so is placed before the doors of churches(templum).

The church bell invites people to heavenly things while the weathercock calls them to daily vigilance. Alciatus maintains that the bell and the weathercock symbolize religious life whose two characteristics are vigilance and purity.

The moral and ethical imports of the sound effect of the bell are to present the purification and change of Alonso which will take place later in the play. His sins are a flaw to the perfection and harmony of the spiritual world of the spirits. In order for his soul to make harmonious music in accordance with the spiritual world it needs to be purified.

The masque scene in IV.i is emblematic in that it is allegorical, moral, and tableau-like. The emblematic meanings of the masque scene are inseparably interlinked with its mode of representation which is clearly distinguished from that of a play. The moral and philosophical imports of the masque scene largely reside in the way it is represented. For this reason the need for a brief examination of the English Renaissance masque arises.

It is not until the Tudor period that the English masque develops to include the dramatic and literary qualities. Before the period the masque remained mainly as a pageant. The introduction of literary elements in the English masque necessitates the invention of form. Enid Welsford comments on the form of the masque as follows:

> Later masques were more elaborate, but with the exception of the antimasque all the elements are here [a masque named *Proteus and the Adamantine Rock*]: the introductory song and dialogue, the entry of the masquers, the masque dances, the revels, the final song and dialogue recalling to the scenes and concluding the performance, and finally the motiving of the whole by a slight story and dramatic action.[13]

The masque scene in *The Tempest* does not fit into this structural principle of the Tudor English masque. The scene lacks elements such as introduction and revels. For this reason the masque scene had better be termed a masque-like play as Miss Welsford explains:

> The attempt to adapt the masque to the requirement of the theater had two chief results . . . . Secondly it led to a loosening of the form of the masque, and consequently to the occasional use of the term as a designation for any masque-like play or entertainment, particularly such as were acted by 'gentlemen of quality' at private houses instead of by players on the public stage.[14]

As a result of the attempt to adapt the masque to plays, the former disintegrated into and was conflated with the latter. The masque is distinguished from the play by criteria such as the status of performers and the kinds of performing places rather than forms and themes. Shakespeare faced the need to employ the mode of representation of the masque in order to create specific effects which are not possibly achieved by the dramatic mode of representation.

One distinctive feature of the masque is that it consists of magnificent and splendid spectacles which create the strong power of vividness. Vivid spectacles make the audience believe what it sees. However, as Ben Jonson remarks in the Introduction to *Hymenaei*, the spectacle is "the transitory device" which "had perished like a blaze and gone out in the beholder's eye."[15] This short-livedness of the spectacle undermines the vividness which temporarily holds the audience under its power. With the spectacle passing away, its vividness vanishes. As Miss Welsford points out, "one of the strong feelings evoked by the masque was a sense of transitoriness and illusion."[16] Based on this we can argue that the sense of pathos felt at the end of the masque stems from this feeling of evanescence.

These two aspects of the masque—evanescence and vividness—provide an important perspective on understanding the masque scene in *The Tempest*. Employing the framework of the masque brings forth the combined effects of vividness and transitoriness. The seeming vivid realness of the pageant turns out to be nothing but a transitory illusiveness. In the masque scene realness and illusiveness are so skillfully infused that the two entities are hardly discernible. The masque scene is realness in illusiveness or illusiveness in realness.

The moral and philosophical question of the masque scene is the ambivalence of ideal pastoralism. At first glance the masque scene appears to celebrate an ideal pastoralism. The pastoral world is that of harmony and order. The vision of harmony is represented by Iris, the goddess of the rainbow, who links the heaven and the earth. Iris welcomes the entrance of Ceres who connotes abundance and riches as well as temperance and prudence. The branches hanging over banks are "pioned and twilled"; the vineyards are "pole-clipt"; the shore is "sterile and rocky-hard." Furthermore, nymphs remain "cold" and "the dismantled bachelor is lasslorn." Fertility and chastity are perfectly harmonized in the earth of Ceres.

The idealism and perfectionism in the masque scene is well illustrated by its banishment of Cupid and Venus. Ceres banishes the god of love and the goddess of beauty from her earth:

> Tell me, heavenly bow,
> If Venus or her son, as thou dost know,
> Do now attend the queen? Since they did plot
> The means that dusky Dis my daughter got,
> Her and her blind boy's scandalled company
> I have forsworn. (86-91)

Ceres discloses her strong antagonism against Cupid and Venus when she is reminded of their abduction of her daughter, Proserpina. The world of Ceres does not admit any traces of passions and desires which may cause misfortunes and troubles, like those seen in Caliban, Stephano, and Trinculo. The earth of Ceres is governed by divine temperance and holiness.

Nevertheless, the vision of the masque runs counter to the world of the island where the passion-torn drunkards and the sin-driven nobles wander. The masque presents an emblematic contrast to the harpy and the banquet scenes where the sinners are driven by gluttony. The masque also forms an antithesis to the hunting scene where the lust-torn drunkards are chastised.

The emblematic hunting scene in IV.i is acted out by the same spirits which appear to the three sinners in the harpy scene and which perform the goddesses and the nymphs in the masque. Prospero and Ariel ride on the spirits which are transformed into dogs and chase the three drunkards— Stephano, Trinculo, and Caliban.

The hunting scene bears a good comparison and contrast with the harpy and the masque scenes. The hunting scene proves itself to be a foil to the masque scene. Contrary to the masque scene which denotes the fragile world of perfect harmony and beauty, the hunting scene signifies the human world of vices and sins. The same spirits, which bless the ideal couple of Ferdinand and Miranda, ruthlessly chastise the three men of sensuality. The former shows sacred love whereas the latter profane or rather bestial one. In addition to this, the hunting scene reminds the audience of the harpy scene. As the harpy scene portrays divine justice, so the hunting scene concerns punishment of bestial love. This becomes obvious when we consider its two parallel scenes.

In the last scene of *The Merry Wives*, Falstaff enters disguised as a hunter named Herne wearing a buck's head. In his soliloquy immediately following his entrance, the character praises sensual love by alluding to the classical transformations of Jupiter into a bull and a swan:

> O powerful love, that in some respects makes a beast a man; in some other, a man a beast. You were also Jupiter, a swan for the love of Leda. O omnipotent love, how near the god drew to the complexion of a goose! A fault done first in the form of a beast— O Jove, a beastly fault—and then another fault in the semblance of a fowl . . . . When gods have hot backs, what shall poor men do? (V.v 4-12)

The rationale of identifying a man and a beast is that both share the desire for satisfying sensual appetite. Even gods assume the forms of animals to gratify their sensual love. Then how much more natural it is for a man to pursue sensual love? However, the playwright of *The Merry Wives* gives moral instruction on sensual love. Falstaff's pursuit of lust endangers his life. He is hunted by the husbands of the wives instead of satisfying his lust. He is punished for his lust by the fairies which the wives impersonate.

The lust-punishing ritual involves the wives' pinching the villain and torturing him with tapers. The fact that lust is a vice to shun is illustrated in the song of the wives:

Fie on sinful fantasy!
Fie on lust and luxury!
Lust is but a bloody-fire,
Kindled with unchaste desire,
Fed in heart, whose flames aspire,
As though do blow them, higher and higher. (V.v 91-96)

The fairy-enacting wives condemns lust as an unchaste sin which arises in the heart. Lust is a "bloody-fire" which intensifies and finally causes destruction.

The myth of Actaeon, which is a possible source of the last scene of *The Merry Wives*, also illustrates the hunting scene. The story of Actaeon's transformation into a stag and his pathetic death by the dogs is an obvious analogy to the episode of the three sensual men chased by the spirits. Importantly in the Renaissance emblem literature the myth often moralizes the danger of base affection as seen in Whitney's emblem 15 (Plate 16):

ACTAEON heare, vnhappie man behoulde,
When in the well, hee sawe Diana brighte,
With greedie lookes, hee waxed ouer boulde,
That to a stagge hee was transformed righte,
    Whereat amasde, hee thought to runne awaie,
    But straight his howndes did rente hym, for their praie.
By which is ment, That those whoe do pursue
Theire fancies fonde, and thinges vnlawfull craue,
Like brutishe beastes appeare vnto the viewe,
And shall at lengte, Actaeons guerdon haue:
    And as his houndes, soe theire affections base,
    Shall them deuowre, and all their deedes deface.

Whitney's moral interpretation of the myth is that those who crave unlawful things are nothing better than beasts and that they are destroyed. He identifies unlawful things to be "affections base," that is lust. This lust devours man as the hounds Actaeon. Lust is compared to the hounds of Diana.

The hunting scene convinces the audience of the dangers of sensual love. The scene condemns bestial or sensual love which is driven by lust. Man is different from animals in that he has reason. Reason enables man to pursue sacred, chaste love. The three drunkards are punished because of their sensual love. Their harsh punishment is incurred by their attempt to rape Miranda. Their blind pursuit of sensual love makes them nothing better than beasts as Caliban ironically comments: "We shall lose our time / And all be turned to barnacles, or to apes / With foreheads villainous low" (IV.i 246-48).

The animal imagery in Caliban's speech mirrors that in Falstaff's in *The Merry Wives*. Caliban's mention of the barnacle echoes the goose which Falstaff mentions in his speech on Jupiter's transformations. It is noteworthy that in II.ii Stephano refers to Trinculo as a goose: "Though thou canst swim like a duck, thou are made like a goose" (127-28). With regard to the ape, Panofsky offers the following iconographic interpretation:

> Now the most common significance of the ape—far more common than its associations with painting, let alone with the other arts and crafts—was a moral one: more closely akin to man in appearance and behavior than any other beast, yet avoid of reason and proverbially prurient (*turpissima bestia, simillima nostri*) the ape was used as a symbol of everything subhuman in man, of lust, greed, gluttony and shamelessness in the widest possible sense.[17]

The ape as a moral emblem signifies subhuman nature such as lust, gluttony, and greed. The ape symbolism in Caliban's speech especially has bearing on lust. The three sensual men degenerate into beasts in a metaphorical sense. By submitting to passion they abandon the nobility of human beings which resides in right exercise of reason. In this light the picture of the three men struggling in the stinky pool is as pungent a satire on the disgusting vices of men as the description of Yahoo in *Gulliver's Travels.*

The emblem and emblematic scenes in *The Tempest* present essential moral and ethical meanings which form the backbone of the play. Shakespeare is fully dextrous in adapting emblems to the theater. For him emblems are a resourceful genre. He, however, continues to experiment with the possibility of introducing another genre, the pageantry, into the drama in *Henry VIII*, which I will discuss in the next chapter.

Notes

1. Stephen Orgel, *The Jonsonian Masque* (New York: Columbia UP, 1981), pp.151-57.
2. Quoted in Stephen Orgel, *The Jonsonian Masque*, p.157.
3. John Doebler, *Shakespeare's Speaking Pictures*, p.152.
4. John Doebler, p.151.
5. The quotation is taken from Virgil, *Aeneid*, trans. Allen Mandelbaum (Berkeley: U of California P. 1971).
6. The Latin phrase is taken from Charles Knapp, ed., *The Aeneid of Vergil and The Metamorphosis of Ovid* (Chicago: Scott, Foresman and Company, 1928), p.294.
7. George Sandys, *Ovid's Metamorphosis Englished, Mythologized, and Represented in Figures*, ed. Karl K. Hulley and Stanley T. Vandersall (Lincoln: U of Nebraska P, 1970), pp.330-31.
8. John Doebler, p.154.
9. John Hollander, *The Untuning of the Sky* (Princeton: Princeton UP, 1961), p.72.

10. J. Dover Wilson, ed., *Life in Shakespeare's England* (London: Penguin, 1959), p.37.

11. The quotation is taken from John Bunyan, *A Book for Boys and Girls, or Country Rhymes for Children*, 1686, intro. John Brown (London: Elliot Stock, 1889).

12. Quoted in John Hollander, pp.279-80.

13. Enid Welsford, *The Court Masque* (New York: Russell and Russell, 1962), pp.163-64.

14. Enid Welsford, pp. 215-16.

15. For the selected anthology of Ben Jonson's masques, see *Ben Jonson: Selected Masques*, ed. Stephen Orgel (New Haven: Yale UP, 1970).

16. Enid Welsford, p.346.

17. Erwin Panofsky, *Studies in Iconology*, p.195.

CHAPTER 6

Henry VIII

In *Henry VIII* Shakespeare employs various kinds of spectacles such as royal entry and the masque. These spectacles have four features.

First, they address political themes instead of merely entertaining the audience. They are incorporated into the play to deliver a political ideology based on the English Tudor myth. He endows the play with the pastoral vision of the Tudor dynasty rather than conferring a sense of historical truth on the audience. The fact that the play world of the play portrays "the mythic realm of a Tudor golden age"[1] qualifies it to be classified as a so-called romance rather than a history. *Henry VIII* fulfills its propagandistic purpose by conveying Tudor political philosophy in the form of shows staged for the public audience. This leads us to the conclusion that in order to fully understand the play, it is crucial to probe into the political symbolism of the spectacles.

Second, they contribute to his experiment with dramatic mode of representation which is grounded on the interaction between actors' speeches and gestures. His concern with the modes of representation leads him to experiment in the other last plays with emblematic modes of representation which

depend on the correlational relationship between the picture
and the poem in the emblem. In *Henry VIII*, however, the
playwright is keenly conscious of introducing the shows into
the drama. As is discussed in *The Tempest*, the playwright is
clearly aware that the shows attract the audience with their
splendor and pomposity. Especially in *Henry VIII* which
deals with the glory and magnificence of Tudor dynasty, the
playwright may have felt the need of arousing the audience's
attention with the aid of the shows.

Third, even though the pageants in *Henry VIII* do not exactly
fit into the three categories of emblems in drama—auditory,
visual, and theater emblems—which I explained in the
introduction, they can be called visual emblems or theater
emblems mainly in that they are allegorical and picturesque. In
a way, the shows are compared to the pictures in emblems.
One of the differences between the emblems and the shows in
drama is that the former are static while the latter dynamic.
Interestingly, their political imports concealed in their
ceremonial showiness are often tacitly provided by presenters
such as the Gentlemen in the coronation scene in IV.i.

Fourth, that Shakespeare exploits another form of art, that
is show, in his play, makes it difficult to distinguish emblem
from emblematic scenes, to whose division I have adhered
up to the last chapter. The several main scenes which I will
focus on in this chapter are divided into two categories
according to whether they are the playwright's own creations
and his adaptations, or his faithful reconstructions mainly
from Holinshed's *Chronicles*. The banquet scene in I.iv, the
trial scenes in II.iv and V.iii, and the vision scene in IV.ii are
classified as the former while the coronation scene in IV.i
and the christening scene in V.v as the latter. Through the
first group of scenes the playwright largely explores the
political idea of divine kingship and royal absolutism. On the
other hand in the second group of scenes he mainly throws

light on the theme of peace and harmony after the nation was torn by the War of the Roses.

Like the masque scene in *The Tempest* the banquet scene in I.iv of *Henry VIII* bears some features of the mask. First the king and others enter the stage wearing the masks. Second, they dance with the ladies who are participants of the banquet as the masquers do in the revels. In spite of the fact that the banquet scene can be classified as the masque, it is safer to call it the water festival called "magnificence," one of the court festivals, or the amalgam of the festival and the masque. The term "magnificence" is derived from the Aristotelian and Thomist idea of magnificence. Both philosophers regard magnificence as the princely virtue which is epitomized in great expenditure. The rationale for this classification is provided by the description made by the servant in the play. Assuming the role of the presenter, he narrates the emergence of the masquers at the request of the lord chamberlain who was surprised by the chamber salute for them: "A noble troop of strangers / For so they seem. Th' have left their barge and landed / And hither make, as great ambassadors / From foreign princess" (54-57). They enter the stage "habited like shepherds, ushered by the lord chamberlain" (I.iv 64-68) at the music of hautboys. Later they ask Wolsey for permission to dance with the ladies present at the banquet.

The servant's narration of the masquers closely runs a parallel to the water festivals celebrated at Fontainbleau and Bayonne in 1564 and 1565 respectively. These French fetes, which form a part of the "magnificence", feature the common pattern of a voyage, a banquet, and a ballet. Catherine de' Medici, queen of Henry II, King of France who ruled from 1547 to 1559, staged these court fetes. The queen organized many water festivals until she died in 1589 for the political purpose of voicing the importance of peace and serenity in a France torn by religious conflicts among rivals. Marguerite, daughter of Catherine de' Medici, depicts the water festival at Bayonne as follows:

> These shepherdesses, during the passage of the superb boats from Bayonne to the island, were placed in separate bands, in a meadow on each side of the causeway, raised with turf . . . . After landing, the shepherdesses I have mentioned before received the company in separate troops, with sinop and dances, after the fashion and accompanied by the music of provinces they represented—the Poiterins playing on bagpipes; the Provençales on the viol and cymbal; the Burgundians and Champagners on the hautboys, bass viol, and tambourine; in like manner the Bretons and other provincialists.[2]

Marguerite draws the similarities between the French fete and the banquet scene in *Henry VIII*: the voyage, the dance, and the music. As shepherdesses in the French fete landed on the island, the masquers in *Henry VIII* arrived in England. The shepherdesses and the masquers alike are welcomed by the music played by instruments such as hautboys. Most importantly, the shepherdesses and the masquers participate in a dance.

The significance of dance in the "magnificence" is clearly seen in the fact that the fete developed into a *ballet de cour* in which a dance plays a leading role. In Renaissance Europe, a dance takes on the meaning of harmony which originated from the idea of correspondence with heavenly sphere, that is, *musica mundana* which I discussed in *The Tempest*. This idea of the harmonious sphere is interlinked with that of the heavenly music. This celestial music is manifested in instrumental music. Later, the idea of harmony in dance and music addresses the political ideology of absolutism as is explicated by Roy Strong:

> Bayonne may seem a very far cry from this theorizing, but by the opening of the next century the dance was to become one of the

most perfect visual vehicles through which to express theories of absolute monarchy. As we follow the development of the use of dance in Valois court festivals, it gradually becomes a way to express the political order of things. By bringing spectators into the chain by the introduction of general dancing after the main ballet, it became the ideal vehicle, in both France and England, for drawing the onlookers into the ideological theme of the spectacle. In this audience participations they 'renewed' themselves and outwardly demonstrated their adherence to the ideal principles of government expounded in the court fête. This was incipient at Bayonne, but it was to be taken a decisive stag further seven years later in the next great series of 'magnificence.' ﹅

According to Strong, the water festival at Bayonne purposes to consolidate the political ideology of absolutism. The spectators experience the absolutist ideology while the audience and the players dance together. As is hinted by Stephen Orgel, Renaissance court festivals were not merely a means of entertainment but a vehicle of political propaganda.[4]

The king's magnificence and liberality are the two pillars of absolutism. Holinshed, the author of *Chronicles*, proposes that the masquers in the banquet scene in *Henry VIII* are all dressed in garments made of fine cloth of gold.[5] The masquers' costume recalls us of the feast of the pageantry of the cloth of gold in the beginning scene. Norfork's narration inspires the audience with the splendor and pomposity of the feast:

> Then you lost
> The view of earthly glory . . . .
> All clinquant, all in gold, like heathen gods
> Shone down the English . . .
> . . . .
> . . . their dwarfish pages were
> As cherubins, all gilt . . . .
> When these suns (For so they phrase 'em) by their heralds
>   challenged
> The noble spirits to arms. (I.i 13-34).

Norfork suggests that the kings are gods and the courtiers cherubins. The splendidness and grandeur of the feast implant awe in the hearts of the beholders and deprive them of any possible criticism of the kings. The monarchs rule their subjects with the magnificence and liberality which are founded on their capability for benevolent expenditure. The repeated expressions, "all in gold" and "all gilt," underscore the magnificence and liberality of the English and French kings as sun kings. Thus, this feast apotheosizes the kings and endows them with the divine power to arbitrate earthly matters.

The feast of the pageantry of the cloth of gold in the beginning scene of *Henry VIII*, which is called the "masque" (26) by Norfolk, possibly stems from the court chivalry which was changed from military training to artistic forms where knights undergo adventures, fight in tournaments with famed warriors, and finally emerge victors. Renaissance monarchs harness the dramatized chivalry to produce the image of a king as an all-time victor and an arbitrator. According to Strong, the feast of the field of cloth is celebrated to create the genuine belief that "the political problems of Europe would be solved if only monarchs met over a conference table and reduced their wars to chivalrous sports."[6] The encounter of Henry VIII and Francis I creates a sufficiently powerful symbol of peace between the two countries.

The absolute monarchy also presupposes the king's moral and cosmic power to restore the fallen world and reinstate order. Monarchs are endowed with the power to restore the pre-lapserian world where all the dangerous potentialities are banished. The king brings back the golden age by changing winter to spring. Moreover, the king performs these functions through his intellect. Orgel states that "the ruler gradually moves from a hero, the center of a court and a culture, to the god of power, the center of a universe."[7] The king is a key note figure who ushers in restored cosmic order. Likewise the king plays a central role in pastoral idealism. In the banquet scene this ideal pastoralism is manifested by the masquers who wear the vizards of shepherds.

Henry VIII as the ideal king with moral and intellectual power is poignantly suggested by the stage description in II.i.60: "the king draws the curtain and sits reading pensively." In Renaissance drama, a book is often adopted as a symbol of the private virtue of contemplative life which constitutes the ideal kingship together with active life. In this way, the book-reading activity creates the image of the prudent Henry. This tableau eradicates the worry of Norfork and Suffolk that he lacks the vision to see Wolsey's scheme to get the king to divorce Katherline and marry the Duchess of Alencon, the sister of Francis I. The cardinal devises the plan partly out of his revenge for the denial by Charles V, Katherline's great nephew, to appoint him archbishop of Toledo and partly out of his desire to maintain his religious power. As both of the courtiers comment, the king's eyes "have slept upon this bold bad man" (41-42). Contrary to their worry, Henry, however, outwits Wolsey. The king's intellectual superiority to the cardinal is visually staged by his act of reading which signifies the power of contemplation and the virtue of prudence. This scene finally paves the way for the king's frowning on the cardinal in III.ii: "Exit king frowning upon the cardinal" (203). From this moment the fortune of the cardinal precipitates down to his end in death. The king so excels in his intellect that he cannot be fooled by the cardinal's knavery and craftiness. The king's turning a cold shoulder on Wolsey in III.ii is a drastic change from the monarch's entering leaning on the cardinal in I.ii. The king, who seems to be vulnerable to the cardinal's manipulating contrivance, overthrows it with his supreme intellectual power.

In *Henry VIII* the king's intellectual power is closely interfused with his political hegemony. The king's rule is founded not only on intellectual faculties but also on political power. The play sheds light on the process of how the king defeats the dominant influence of Catholicism in the English court and the society, and succeeds in establishing his kingship as the head of the English state and the church. Unlike the kings of other European countries, Henry treated the Church as a simple political constitution and subjugated it under English kingship "as a part and parcel of the realm of England."[8] These political implications of kingship are mainly dealt with in the trial scenes for the four leading figures: Buckingham, Katherline, Wolsey, and Cranmer. Among the four, the trial scenes for Katherline in II. iv and Cranmer in V. ii highlight the theme of kingship. The former scene is embedded in the royal session held in Blackfriars on June 18, 1529. This royal session begins with the dumb show and then follows the trial where Katherine is examined by the judges, Cardinal Wolsey, and Campeius. Much of the council-chamber scene for Cranmer is derived and expanded from Foxe's *Acts and Monuments* (1563) but the dramatist's own dramatization is also added.

The royal session in II.iv is slightly modified from the source, Holinshed's *Chronicles*. The historian records that Henry sits in the chamber under the cloth of estate, and Katherline does as well with some distance from the king, while the judges sit on seat raised higher than that for the king.[9] However. The dramatist of *Henry VIII* alters the historian's description by placing the judges on seat under the king. The stage description in the scene sketches the placement of the characters as follows: "the king takes place under the cloth of state; the two cardinals sit under him as judges. The queen takes some place some distance from the king." The arrangement of the seats for the king and the cardinals poses a significant political meaning which is crucial in understanding the play. The vertical position of the king and the cardinals indicates the power relationship between them. Unlike Holinshed, Shakespeare tacitly emphasizes that the king occupies the central place which is on a higher level than the seat for the cardinals. This spatial codes convey the message that the king is more powerful than the church leaders though he and the queen stand trial before them. The position of the king on the stage visually implies that the king is in control of the trial and the judges. This rivalry between the head of state and the high-ranking churchmen is seen in their contention over the issue of divorce. The king voices his antagonism toward the cardinals in his aside at the end of the session: "These cardinals trifle with me: I abhor / This dilatory sloth and tricks of Rome (232-33)." Requesting the judges to continue the session, Henry asks them to pronounce his marriage to Katherline, the widow of his deceased brother Prince Arthur, unlawful so that he can divorce her. But the judges adjoin the session on the ground that Katherline is absent. The struggle for the hegemony between the English state and the Roman church remains at equilibrium.

In the final act, the king exercises his hegemony over the church by keeping the church under his power. The king's supremacy over the church is visually represented by the two tableaus. The first is his entering the stage with Butts "at a window above" (20) in V.ii. The king looks down at the council members who convene for the trial of Cranmer accused of spreading heresy. The trial is a clash between Roman Catholicism and Protestantism. As an archbishop of Canterbury, Cranmer is an ardent advocate of Protestantism, and he poses a threat to Roman Catholicism. The higher position of the king on the vertical scale than that of the council members dramatically expresses that he has subjugated the Catholic group under his rule contrary to their allegation of a king's temporal sovereignty. The king's domination of the Roman church is more poignantly conveyed by the following scene where the king frowns at the members of the trial. The following stage description is worth noting: "A council table brought in with chairs and stools, and placed under the state." Here the state means the throne and according to Martha Fleischer, the king "takes his seat at the head of the table 'frowning on them.'"[10] As the stage description verifies ("Gardiner seat themselves in order on each side"), the council observes the traditionally strict seating order. This state scene is a static visual emblem of Henry's rule over the church. Henry clarifies this by reminding them that he confers the power to judge Cranmer on them: "Why, what a shame was this? Did my commission / Bid ye so far forget yourselves? I gave ye / Power as he was a councilor to try him" (V.ii 141-43). As he gives the council the judicial power, so he has the authority to acquit Cranmer.

The second tableau representing the state's rule over the church is Cranmer's kneeling down at the feet of Henry in the beginning of V.v. The head of the protestant church, who is martyred in the reign of Mary queen of Scots (1542-87), pays tribute to Henry, and Elizabeth. As Cox observes, Henry is a mouthpiece for James I who struggled against both Roman Catholicism and Puritanism which denied his absolute power.[11] The dramatist of *Henry VIII* plainly demonstrates that Henry is the head of the church and the state both through the actors' gestures and speeches. As is proved in the coronation and the baptism scenes, which I will discuss in the next sections, Henry unmistakably speaks up for James I who was the patron of the King's Men. In James I's reign absolute monarchy reaches its peak and the two tableau scenes deliver pregnant political and religious messages both to the Jacobean audience and the king.

The political idea of ideal kingship and royal absolutism in the banquet and the trial scenes recurs in the coronation scene in IV.i which took place in 1533. The progress is staged not merely for the sake of pleasing the audience, but for the sake of conveying political signification. Royal entries and pageantry assume dynastic apotheosis rather than secular entertainment. The gentleman, who performs the function of a presenter, discloses that the purpose of the pageantry is to express "general joy" (IV.i 7). The general joy of the scene arises from the fact that "she [Anne Boleyn] had all the royal makings of a queen, / As holy oil Edward Confessor crown, / The rod, and bird of peace, and all such emblems / Laid nobly on her" (87-90). As Henry is an ideal king, so Anne Boleyn is a perfect queen. Holinshed describes this ceremony as follows:

> the bishop anointed hir on the head and on the breast . . . . the archbishop set the crown of Saint Edward on hir head, and then delivered hir the scepter of gold in hir right hand, and the rod of ivorie with the dove in the left hand, and then all the queere soong *Te Deum*.[12]

It is interesting to notice that in the historical coronation procession Anne Boleyn is presented with a series of golden gifts denoting the golden age which will come upon her coronation: "gold coins, Paris's golden apple, a gift of golden verses, the golden crown of a queen.[13] Based on Holinshed, the golden age of Anne Boleyn is distinguished by two aspects: holiness and peace. As a royal partner for Henry who wields absolute power, Anne Boleyn is sanctified for two reasons. First, that Anne Boleyn was the handmaid of Katherline, the former queen, calls for the apotheosis of the new queen so that she may be an equal match for the king. Second, in political absolutism the king is likened to the sun and the queen is deified in the same way. As a result she can be free from the possible charges against her for ascending the throne at the sacrifice of Katherine. Through the coronation procession, Anne Boleyn is endowed with these qualities. The royal spectacle functions to publicly proclaim this. She is acknowledged as the source of all spiritual and material blessings as evinced in this statement by the Second Gentleman:

> Heaven bless thee,
> Thou has the sweetest face I ever looked on.
> Sir, as I have a soul, she is an angel;
> Our king has all the Indies in his arms,
> And more, and more richer, when he strains that lady. (IV.i 42-46).

The new queen is also portrayed as a harbinger of peace. When we are reminded that she was confronted with the danger of being branded as the cause of discord in England over Henry's divorce from Katherline, it is quite natural for Shakespeare to sketch her as the Queen of Peace. The peace the newly anointed queen brings forth is poignantly vented by the crowd's joy in celebrating the coronation with one mind. Even "great-bellied women," who "had not half a week to go (76-77)," participated in the ceremony and they are "woven in so strangely in one piece" (IV.i 79-80). The bitter conflicts arising from the divorce issue among the people disappear during the coronation festival. The new queen consolidates this newly cemented peace. The image of the peaceful queen echoes in James I's own motto, "*Beati Pacifici*," which is translated as "blessed peace."

While in IV.i Anne Boleyn is crowned as the earthly queen of England, Katherline of Aragon wears her heavenly crown in IV.ii. In this way, the former foreshadows the latter and this parallelism signifies that the latter is the spiritual version of the former. The interpretative framework for the former coronation scene is also applicable to the latter vision scene.

When Foakes comments that the vision scene is "heavenly
coronation"[14], he means that the scene is not so much pathetic
as felicitous as is hinted through Katherine's comment that it
is the "banquet" (88). The two queens share in the queenship
of peace and holiness. As Katherline's queenship is
celebrated in the vision scene, so Anne Boleyn's queenship is
honored in the coronation scene. With regard to the heavenly
queenship of the deposed queen, Kipling provides us with
the invaluable description of the historical coronation
pageantry for her:

> The anonymous dramatist who designed Katherline of Aragon's
> triumph, for example, cast her as the heroine of a medieval dream
> vision. By carefully structuring the princess's pageant encounters,
> he makes Katherline travel from earth, through the sphere of the
> cosmos, to an apotheosis upon the Throne of Honor above the
> firmament.[15]

There are striking affinities between the historical
coronation triumph and the vision scene in *Henry VIII*. First,
both the triumph and the "vision" share the same features of
dream vision. As the former expresses Katherline's dream in
the form of a pageant, so the latter represents her dream in
the form of a mask. The fact that the latter is a dream vision
is underlined by the stage description: "she makes (in her
sleep) signs of rejoicing and holdeth up her hands to
heaven." Second, both the pageant and the mask present her
as the heroine of virtue. These correspondences lead us to
assume that the dramatist of *Henry VIII* models the vision
scene on the coronation triumph for Katherline. Whether this
assumption is verified or not, it is quite convincing to
conclude that the allegorical meaning of the vision scene can
be supplied by the coronation pageantry.

The "vision" delivers the audience the moral lessons of
heavenly glory and earthly virtue. Unearthing these moral

lessons requires to identify "the six personages clad in white robes, wearing the garlands of bays." Interestingly, these figures resemble the mythological figure of graces and hours. When Queen Elizabeth entered into the estate of the Earl of Herford at Elvetham in 1591, a pageant was performed. In this spectacle six virgins engaged themselves in preparing the way for the queen by removing the blocks representative of vices which were laid before her. Bergeron maintains that "these virgins represent the mythological Graces and Hours which by the poets are fained to be the guardians of heaven gates."[16] Bergeron continues to claim that these virgins correspond to the graces in Botticeli's *Primavera* (Plate 13) which I discussed in *The Winter's Tale*. Botticeli's graces are "attired in gowns of taffata sarcenet of divers colours, with flowerie garlands on their heads, and baskets full of sweet hearbs and flowers upon their arms."[17] Extending this analogy Katherline can be identified with *Flora*, the goddess of flowers. This identification becomes more plausible when taking into account that in English pageantry a queen is often regarded as the goddess of flowers.[18] Based on the parallels between the graces in the Elvetham entry and the six personages in the vision scene, we can draw the conclusion that the latter figures are the spiritual agents who perform the heavenly coronation for Katherline.

The dramatist of *Henry VIII* carves out Katherline's moral virtues through several attributes. The garland is an emblem of "earthly virtue and heavenly glory."[19] In his emblem 258 (Plate 17) whose motto is "The Garland He alone shall weare / Who, to the Goale, doth preservere," George Wither interprets the garland as the symbol of heavenly reward for those who preserve. The epigram clarifies that "An arme is with a garland here extended; / And, as the Motto saith, it is intended, / To all that persevere" (1-3). Katherline's remark after the vision scene unravels that the personages bring her happiness and contentment:

Saw you not a blessed troop
Invite me to a banquet whose bright faces
Cast thousand beams upon me like the sun
They promised me eternal happiness and broght me garlands. (87-90).

This spiritual lesson is further reinforced by the unmistakable symbolic meaning of Patience, the queen's page. As Roy Walker observes, Patience accomplishes her full dramatic implication when she is represented as an angel waiting on her, while Griffith, gentleman usher to her, as the figure of charity.[20]

As the presenter of the vision scene, Katherline pinpoints another level of meaning by alluding to the six personages as the "spirit of peace" (IV.i 83). The image of the figures as the spirit of peace is emblematized by the garlands of bays on their heads, and the branches of bays or palm in their hands. This portrayal parallels the personification of peace given by Cesare Ripa. According to the iconographer, Peace is "a winged young woman dressed in white, with a wreath of grain and olive on her head and a palm frond tucked under her arm."[21] The six personages in the "vision" are analogous to Ripa's Peace in that the former wear white robes and have branches of palm in their hands.

Like the banquet, trial, coronation, and vision scenes, the baptism scene also delivers political themes. This concluding scene underscores the national issues of union and harmony which will be achieved by the rule of Elizabeth, the high and mighty princess of England. The birth of Elizabeth foretells the appearance of the ideal queenship which is partly embodied in Anne Boleyn and the late queen Katherline. The christening is representative of birth and renewal for the nation torn by conflict. As a future monarch, Elizabeth is born with queenly graces and virtues which will promise the nation unprecedented prosperity. In this way the baptism scene is not merely a progress entertaining the audience but an emblematic scene containing political symbolism.

This political symbolism is intimated by Cranmer who plays the role of a presenter. Cranmer employs the metaphors of the phoenix and the vine to deliver this symbolism. In the speech following the baptism, the archbishop prophesies that the blessings of Elizabeth will not disappear on her death, but extend to James I as the phoenix revives from the ash of its death and the vine grows climbing over a wall:

> Nor shall this peace sleep with her; but as when
> The bird of wonder dies, the maiden phoenix,
> Her ashes new create another heir
> As great in admiration as herself,
> So shall she leave her blessedness to one
> . . . .
> Who from the sacred ashes of her honor
> Shall starlike rise, as great in fame as she was,
> And so stand fixed. Peace, plenty, love, truth, terror,
> That were the servants to this chosen infant,
> Shall then be his, and like a vine grow to him. (40-49)

Cranmer observes that the political ideology of Elizabethan rule is epitomized in terms such as "peace," "plenty," "love," "truth," and "terror." This Elizabethan governing principles revive in the succeeding monarchs as the phoenix rises from the ashes of its death. It is worth while to note that the phoenix was "a personal badge of Queen Elizabeth signifying her virginity as well as her singularity: *sola phoenix* is the inscription on some of her coins, and as *unica phoenix* she is celebrated in a medallion issued in the year of her demise, 1603."[22] In Emblem III of Sir Henry Godyere's *The Mirror of Majestie; or, The Badge of Honour* (1618),[23] whose motto is *unica eterna al mondo* ("unique and eternal in all years"), the queen is compared to the phoenix because of her matchlessness, unparalleledness, and uniqueness. Importantly Charles I and II also adopted the mythological bird as their personal badges.[24] This historical facts have bearing on the bird's political symbolism on which Martha Fleischer comments as follows: "it [the phoenix] also symbolizes the perpetual life, the official resurrection of kingship, . . . in accordance with the traditional cry, 'The king is dead. Long live the king.'"[25]

The political allegory of the phoenix is interfused with that of the vine. After the hundred years' war, England was faced with the imminent issue of uniting the divided nation. This national mandate is voiced by the symbols of the phoenix and the vine. In the late summer of 1578, Queen Elizabeth made a procession throughout Suffolk and Norfolk. On August 16 the queen paid a royal visit to Norwich where a special pageant was presented. As a part of the procession, the queen entered St. Stephen's Gate, whose indoor decoration Holinshed describes in the following:

> On the right side was gorgeouslie set foorth the red rose, signifieing the house of Yorke[sic]; on the left side the white rose, representing the house of Lancaster[sic]; in the midet was the white and red rose united, expressing the union. . .[26]

The allegorical import of this device is rendered clear by the verse under it:

> Division kindled strife,
> Blist union quench the flame:
> Thence sprang our noble Phenix deare,
> The pearlesss prince of fame. [27]

Henry VIII and Queen Anne Boleyn constitute a genealogical tree which emblematizes the union of the nation. From this union, the new baby will be born as a phoenix which will outstrip the division. The aspiration of the national unity, which rang the nation from Henry VII to James I, is fulfilled in the person of Queen Elizabeth.

In addition Cranmer employs the image of the lily for

Queen Elizabeth along with those of the vine and the phoenix:

> Would I had known no more! but she must die,
> She must, the saints must have her: yet a virgin,
> A most unspotted lily shall she pass
> To th' ground, and all the world shall mourn her. (V.v 59-62).

The lily stands for Queen Elizabeth's personal virtues such as chastity and humility as seen in Henry Hawkins' s emblem 3 on the lily in *Partheneia Sacra*. The motto of the emblem is *ego dilecto meo qui pascitur inter lilia*, which means that "I am delighted with myself who can be nourished by the lily." The poem goes as follows:

> *A pure-white* lillie, *like a siluer Cup,*
> *The sacred* Virgin *humbly offers vp.*
> *Her constant, stedfast, lowelie* Hart *(the foot,*
> *Which al supports) is like this flower's root.*
> *The stemme, her right* Intention; *& the bole*
> *(The flower itself) is her chast spotlesse* Soule,
> *The yellow knobbes, which sprowing forth are seen,*
> *Is radiant* Loue, *which guild's her Cup within.*
> *In lieu of liquides, is a fragrant sent:*
> *Her vertues odours, which she doth present.*
> *Her sonne accepts al, that she offers vp,*
> God, *Part of her inheritance, & Cup.* [28]

The epigram divides the flower into three parts and connects each of them with singular virtues. The root, which supports the flower, signifies the Virgin's constancy, steadfastness, and humility, while the stem, which straightly ascends, her right intention. Lastly, the bowl connotes her chastity. Interestingly the Queen is praised for her holiness as were Katherline and Anne Boleyn. Nevertheless Queen Elizabeth is distinguished from the latter queens by her chastity. Queen Elizabeth is likened to the Virgin Mary due to her chastity. This Elizabeth-Mary analogy vests the queen with the divine power to rule her people. This is the rationale for them to worship her. The absolute kingship, which is based on the idea of god-given power, is clearly manifested in the person of Queen Elizabeth through this analogy. In the baptism scene, the dramatist of *Henry VIII* loudly pays tribute to the rule of the deceased Elizabeth and the incumbent James I, whose kingship is also founded on ideas such as peace, plenty, love, truth, and terror.

In *Henry VIII*, Shakespeare probes into the question of ideal kingship which is inseminated in the reign of King Henry VIII, flowers in the rule of Queen Elizabeth, and finally culminates in the government of James I. This period sees the foundation of absolute kingship, and this political ideology is powerfully conveyed to the audience through grandiose spectacles such as masks and triumphs. These pageants cease to be mere entertainments, but function as a kind of visual emblem. These emblems are quite different from the theater emblems in the other last plays. First the former are historical re-presentations with the exception of the "vision" and the banquet scenes, while the latter offers dramatic representations of emblems on the stage. Second, the former are shows while the latter emblems on the stage. Both of the shows in *Henry VIII* and emblems in the other plays, however, are impregnated with allegorical and symbolic meanings and depend on the dynamics between the actors' gesture and their speeches for representation. In this sense, *Henry VIII* is grouped together with the other plays— *Pericles, Cymbeline, The Winter's Tale, and The Tempest*—as the last plays. They are alike classified as one group of plays which are concerned with the mode of representation, and are filled with moral and philosophical lessons.

One of the possible reasons why Shakespeare are deeply steeped in emblems and shows in the last plays is that he holds on to the belief that the reality of life and history depends on how we see them, not on what they are. Throughout the last plays, Shakespeare is more inclined to this nonmimetic or romantic vision of life and history than to mimetic, or rather realistic vision. Especially in *Henry VIII* Shakespeare sheds light on this romantic perspective on history by examining pageantry as a new possible mode of dramatic representation, and as a forceful channel for delivering political imports.

Notes

1. Howard Felperin, *Shakespearean Romance* (Princeton: Princeton UP, 1972), p. 208.
2. Quoted in Roy Strong, *Splendor at Court* (Boston: Houghton Mifflin, 1973), p. 138.
3. Roy Strong, pp. 140-41.
4. Stephen Orgel, *The Illusion of Power* (Berkeley: U of California P, 1991), p. 8.
5. William Shakespeare, *King Henry VIII*, ed. R. Foakes (London: Methuen, 1964), p. 204.
6. Roy Strong, *Splendor at Court*, p. 44.
7. Stephen Orgel, *The Illusion of Power*, p. 52.
8. Ernst Kantorowicz, *The King's Two Bodies* (New Jersy: Princeton UP, 1957), p. 229.
9. *King Henry VIII*, ed. R. Foakes, p. 194.
10. Martha Fleischer, *The Iconography of the English History Play* (Salzburg, Austria: Universität Salzburg, 1974), p. 60.
11. John Cox, "*Henry VIII* and the Masque," *English Literary History* 45 (1978): 400.
12. *King Henry VIII*, ed. R. Foakes, p. 209.
13. Gordon Kipling, "Triumphal Drama: Form in English Civic Pageantry," *Renaissance Drama* n.s. 8 (1977): 47.
14. *King Henry VIII*, ed. R. Foakes, p. lii.
15. Gordon Kipling, p. 45.
16. David Bergeron, *English Civic Pageantry: 1558-1642* (Columbia, South Carolina: U of South Carolina P, 1971), p. 58.

17. David Bergeron, p. 58.

18. Stephen Orgel, *The Illusion of Power*, p. 52.

19. Martha Fleischer, *The Iconography of the English History Play*, p. 66.

20. Roy Walker, "The Whirligig of Time: A Review of Recent Production," *Shakespeare Survey* 12 (1959): 125.

21. Cesare Ripa, *Iconologia*, 1593, ed. Erna Mandowsky (Hildesheim, New York: G. Olms, 1970), p. 79.

22. Ernst Kantorowicz, *The King's Two Bodies* (New Jersy: Princeton UP, 1957), p. 413.

23. Modern edition of Henry Godyere is Henry Godyere, *The Mirrour of Majestie*, 1618, ed. Henry Green and James Croston (London, 1870).

24. Ernst Kantorowicz, p. 414.

25. Martha Fleischer, pp. 193-94.

26. Quoted in David Bergeron, p. 38.

27. Quoted in David Bergeron, p. 38.

28. *Partheneia Sacra*, p.35.

CHAPTER 7

Summary and Conclusions

Shakespeare's concern with the mode of representation in drama is attested by the statue scene in *The Winter's Tale*. He was consistently interested in this question at least throughout the last plays. The emblematic representation could lend aid to the playwright. The emblem parallels drama in terms of structure. As the emblem is composed of the picture and the poem, so the drama comprises actors' speeches and gestures. This structural similarity between an emblem and drama makes it possible to adopt the former in the latter. In drama actors's speeches convey *subscriptio* (poem) whereas stage imagery[1] creates *pictura* (picture).

More importantly the emblem can bring in a new aspect, that is, representation and interpretation. Albrecht Schöne, a modern German emblem theorist, sees the functional relationship between the picture and the poem as that of description and explanation:

> The dual function of representation and interpretation, description and explanation, which the tripartite construction of the emblem assumes, is based upon the fact that that which is depicted means more than it portrays. The *res picta* of the emblem is endowed with the power to refer beyond itself; it is a *res significans*.[2]

Schöne stresses that the emblem picture means more than it portrays. In other words there are levels of meaning in the picture. The picture has an allegorical meaning as well as a literal one. The poem comments on these levels of meanings.

The emblematic representation lies in this function of description and explanation. The playwright is conscious of the contributions it can make to drama. When adopted in drama, it produces the provoking and inspiring function of description and explanation between actors' speeches and stage imagery. The relationship between the verbal and visual factors does not remain static but dynamic. The former does not merely explicate the latter as the latter does not simply signify the former. The reciprocal functions of hearing and sight are more than the mere addition of the two. They complement each other.

The fact that the playwright is attracted to the emblematic representation is certainly seen in *Pericles*. The play experiments with verbal presentation (Gower's choruses) and visual presentation (dumb shows). The playwright's effort to exploit the dual function of description and explanation culminates in *The Tempest*. For instance, the harpy and hunting scenes convince us of the debt the playwright owes to the emblematic representation. In *Henry VIII* the playwright continues to experiment with the pageantry with regard to its relation to dramatic representation. Shakespeare's concern in *Henry VIII* with the show, which can be traced back to the masque scene in *The Tempest,* results in conveying political meanings in a splendid and pompous way. The playwright's knowledge of emblems and pageants enables him to harness them in drama.

Emblems also supply Shakespeare with moral ideas which he wants to deliver to the audience. The playwright uses emblems as a means of instructing the audience in a pleasant way. They provide significant ethical and philosophical imports of the last plays.

On a surface level the last plays seem to present "old wives' tales" which lack the seriousness and realness found in tragedies. The plays, however, are impregnated with allegorical and symbolic meanings underlying literal ones. As "sentences" and "expressions" lurk behind seemingly trivial and childish pictures of emblems, so the playwright's vital thematic concerns are embedded in the fairy tale-like stories of the last plays. When we accept the last plays at face value, we miss these important layers of meaning. The multifaceted aspect may go unnoticed. This study calls our attention to these multiple imports of the last plays. If we interpret the headless man episode in *Cymbeline* to address only the theme of appearance and reality, we run the risk of missing its allegorical rendering of reason and passion. This is also true of the bear scene in *The Winter's Tale* and the harpy scene in *The Tempest*. We discover the philosophical question of fate when we pay attention to the allegorical aspect of the bear scene. We find the moral question of divine justice when we are conscious of the symbolic meaning of the scene. We are further awakened to the political ideas of ideal kingship and royal absolutism the banquet and trial scenes in *Henry VIII* when we carefully direct our attention to their political layers of import beneath the literal and historical ones.

A full understanding of the last plays as a whole is not possible without the knowledge of emblems in relation to their structure and morals. This study is an attempt to approach the last plays from this perspective.

Notes

1. This is Martha Fleischer's term. She defines that "stage imagery is created by the persons, proprieties, and actions visible and audible on stage when a play is in production. Its function is analogous to that of allegorical picture in the emblem books of the Renaissance: to present the essential truth for instantaneous comprehension by the eye" (*The Reader's Encyclopedia of Shakespeare*, ed. Oscar James Campbell and Edward G. Quinn [New York: Crowell, 1966]). Unlike Fleischer, I argue that stage imagery is symbolic and is not so easy as to be comprehended instantaneously.

2. Quoted in Peter Daly, *Literature in the Light of Emblem* (Toronto: U of Toronto P, 1979), p. 38.

List of References

Allen, Don Cameron. *Mysteriously Meant: The Rediscovery of Pagan Symbolism and Allegorical Interpretation in the Renaissance.* Baltimore: The Johns Hopkins UP, 1970.

Barber, C. L. *Shakespeare's Festive Comedy: A Study of Dramatic Form and its Relation to Social Custom.* Cleveland: The World Publishing Company, 1963.

Bunyan, John. *A Book for Boys and Girls.* 1686. Intro. John Brown. London: Elliot Stock, 1889.

Clements, Robert. *Michelangelo's Theory of Art.* New York: Gramercy Publishing Company, 1961.

Bergeron, *David M. English Civic Pageantry: 1558-1642.* Columbia, South Carolina: U of South Carolina P, 1971.

Combe, Thomas. *The Theater of Fine Devices.* 1614. San Marino, Cal.: The Huntington Library, 1983.

Cox, John H. "*Henry VIII* and the Masque." *English Literary History* 45 (1978): 390-409.

Daly, Peter. *Literature in the Light of Emblem: Structural Parallels between the Emblem and Literature in the Sixteenth and Seventeenth Century.* Toronto: U of Toronto P, 1979.

___, et al., eds. *Andreas Alciatus*. 2 vols. Toronto: U of Toronto P, 1985.

___, ed. *The English Emblem and the Continental Tradition*. New York: AMS, 1988.

Daniel, Samuel, trans. *The Worthy Tract of Paulus Jovius*. London, 1585.

Diehl, Huston, ed. *An Index of Icons in English Emblem Books: 1500-1700*. Norman: U of Oklahoma P, 1986.

Doebler, John. *Shakespeare's Speaking Pictures: Studies in Iconic Imagery*. Albuquerque, N. M.: U of New Mexico P, 1974.

Fairchild, Arthur H. P. *Shakespeare and the Arts of Design: Architecture, Sculpture, and Painting*. University of Missouri Studies, 12. No. 1. Columbia: U of Missouri P, 1937.

Felperin, Howard. *Shakespearean Romance*. Princeton: Princeton UP, 1972.

Fleischer, Martha Hester. *The Iconography of the English History Play*. Elizabethan and Renaissance Studies. Salzburg, Austria: Universität Salzburg, 1974.

___. "Stage Imagery." *The Reader's Encyclopedia of Shakespeare*. Ed. Oscar James Campbell and Edward G. Quinn. New York: Crowell, 1966.

Foakes, R. A., ed. *King Henry VIII*. The Arden Shakespeare. London: Methuen, 1964.

Fraser, Russell A. and Norman Rabkin, eds. *Drama of the English Renaissance*. 2 vols. New York: Macmillan, 1976.

Freeman, Rosemary. *English Emblem Books*. New York: Octagon, 1966.

Godyere, Henry. *The Mirror of Majestie; or, the Badge of Honour*. London, 1618.

Gombrich, Ernst H. *Symbolic Images: Studies in the Art of the Renaissance*. London: Phaidon, 1972.

Green, Henry, ed. Whitney's *"Choice of Emblemes."* London: Lovell Reeve, 1866.

Gurr, Andrew. "The Bear, the Statue, and Hysteria in *The Winter's Tale.*" *Shakespeare Quarterly* 34 (1983): 420-25.

Harbage, Alfred. *William Shakespeare: The Complete Works.* New York: Viking, 1969.

Hawkins, Henry. *Partheneia Sacra: Or the Mysterious and Delicious Garden of the Sacred Parthenes.* 1633. Ed. John Horden. English Emblem Book No. 10. Menston: The Scolar Press, 1971.

Heckscher, William S. "Shakespeare in His Relationship to the Visual Arts: A Study in Paradox." *Research Opportunities in Renaissance Drama* 13-14 (1970-1971): 5-72.

Holbein, Hans. *The Dance of Death.* Ed. James M. Clark. London: Phaidon, 1947.

Hollander, John. *The Untuning of the Sky: Ideas of Music in English Poetry, 1500-1700.* Princeton: UP, 1961.

Kantorowicz, Ernst H. *The King's Two Bodies: A Study in Medieval Political Theology.* New Jersy: Princeton UP, 1957.

Katzenellenbogen, Adolf. *Allegories of The Virtues and Vices in Medieval Art: From Early Christian Times to the Thirteenth Century.* New York: Norton, 1964.

Kipling, Gordon. "Triumphal Drama: Form in English Civic Pageantry. *Renaissance Drama* n.s. 8 (1977): 37-56.

Knapp, Charles, ed. *The Aeneid of Vergil and The Metamorphosis of Ovid.* The Lake Classical Series. Chicago: Scott, Foresman and Company, 1928.

Knight, G. Wilson. *The Crown of Life.* London: Methuen, 1965.

Ludwig, Jay B. "Shakespearean Decorum: An Essay on *The Winter's Tale.*" *Style* 8:2 (1974): 365-404.

Marston, John. *The Poems of John Marston*. Ed. Alexander Grosart. Manchester, 1879.

Milton, John. *John Milton: Complete Poems and Major Prose*. Ed. Merritt Y. Hughes. Indianapolis: Bobbs-Merrill Educational Publishing, 1984.

Orgel, Stephen, ed. *Ben Jonson: Selected Masques*. New Haven: Yale UP, 1970.

___. *The Jonsonian Masque*. New York: Columbia UP, 1981.

___. *The Illusion of Power: Political Theater in the English Renaissance*. Berkeley: U of California P, 1991.

Owen, John Issac, ed. An Edition of *The Rare Triumphs of Love and Fortune*. New York: Garland Publishing, 1979.

Panofsky, Erwin. *Studies in Iconology: Humanistic Themes in the Art of Renaissance*. New York: Harper and Row, 1962.

Peacham, Henry. *Minerva Britanna, or a Garden of Heroical Devices*. 1612. Leeds, England: The Scolar Press, 1966.

Peterson, Douglas. *Time, Tide, and Tempest: A Study of Shakespeare's Romances*. San Marino, Cal.: The Huntington Library, 1973.

Rhoads, Diana Akers. *Shakespeare's Defense of Poetry: A Midsummer Night's Dream and The Tempest*. Lanham: University Press of America, 1985.

Ripa, Cesare. *Iconologia*. 1593. Ed. Erna Mandowsky. Hildesheim, New York: G. Olms, 1970.

___. *Baroque and Rococo Pictorial Imagery: The 1758-60 Hertel Edition of Ripa's 'Iconologia.'* Ed. and trans. Edward Maser. New York: Dover, 1971.

S., P. *Heroicall Devises . . . of M. Claudius Paradin*. 1591. Delmar, New York: Scholars' Facsimiles and Reprints, 1984.

Salingar, Leo. *Shakespeare and the Traditions of Comedy*. Cambridge: Cambridge UP, 1974.

Sandys, George. *Ovid's Metamorphosis Englished, Mythologized, and Represented in Figures.* Ed. Karl K. Hulley and Stanley T. Vandersall. Lincoln: U of Nebraska P, 1970.

Seznec, Jean. *The Survival of the Pagan Gods: The Mythological Tradition and Its Place in Renaissance Humanism and Art.* Trans. Barbara F. Sessions. Bollingen Series, 38. New York: Pantheon, 1953.

Shakespeare, William. *The Winter's Tale.* Ed. J. H. P. Pafford. The Arden Shakespeare. London: Methuen, 1963.

___. *Pericles.* Ed. F. D. Hoeniger. The Arden Shakespeare. London: Methuen, 1963.

Sidney, Philip. *A Defence of Poetry.* Ed. J. A. Van Dorsten. Oxford: UP, 1966.

Spenser, Edmund. *Spenser: Poetical Works.* Ed. J. C. Smith and E. De Selincourt. Oxford: UP, 1912.

Steadman, John M. "Iconography and Renaissance Drama: Ethical and Mythological Themes." *Research Opportunities in Renaissance Drama* 13-14 (1970-71): 73-122.

Strong, Roy. *Splendor at Court: Renaissance Spectacle and the Theater of Power.* Boston: Houghton Mifflin, 1973.

Tayler, Edward William. *Nature and Art in Renaissance Literature.* New York: Columbia UP, 1964.

Van der Noot, Jan. *A Theatre wherein be represented the miseries that follow the voluptuous worldlings.* London, 1569.

Virgil. *The Aeneid.* Trans. Allen Mandelbaum. Berkeley: U of California P, 1971.

Walker, Roy. "The Whirligig of Time: A Review of Recent Production." *Shakespeare Survey* 12 (1959): 122-30.

Welsford, Enid. *The Court Masque: A Study in the Relationship between Poetry and the Revels.* 1927. New York: Russell and Russell, 1962.

Willet, Andrew. *Sacrorum emblematum centuria una.* London, 1592.

Williams, Kathleen. "Spenser: Some Uses of the Sea and the Storm-tossed Ship." *Research Opportunities in Renaissance Drama* 13-14 (1970-71): 135-42.

Wilson, John Dover, ed. *Life in Shakespeare's England: A Book of Elizabethan Prose.* London: Penguin, 1959.

Wither, George. *A Collection of Emblems.* 1635. Ed. John Horden. English Emblem Studies No. 12. Menston: The Scolar Press, 1968.

Plates

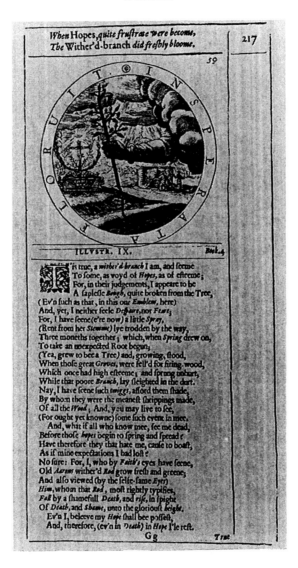

PLATE 1 *Insperata floruit*, from Wither's *A Collection of Emblemes* (1635), emblem no. 217. Reproduced by courtesy of Glasgow University Library, Department of Special Collections.

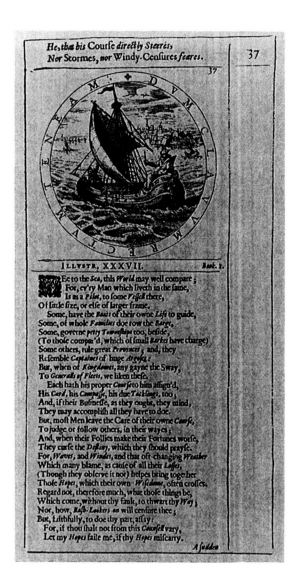

PLATE   2 *Dum clavvm rectvm teneam*, from Wither's *A Collection of Emblemes*(1635), emblem no. 37. Reproduced by courtesy of Glasgow University Library, Department of Special Collections.

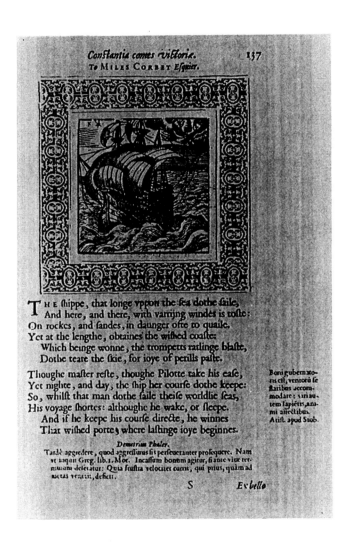

PLATE 3 *Constantia comes victoriae*, from Whitney's *A Choice of Emblemes* (Leyden, 1586), emblem no. 137. Reproduced by courtesy of Glasgow University Library, Department of Special Collections.

PLATE 4 *Manet immvtabile fatvm*, from Wither's *A Collection of Emblemes* (1635), emblem no. 95. Reproduced by courtesy of Glasgow University Library, Department of Special Collections.

PLATE 5 Angelo Bronzino. *Allegory of Luxury* (ca. 1546). Painting. The
National Gallery, London. Reproduced by courtesy of the
Trustees, The National Gallery, London.

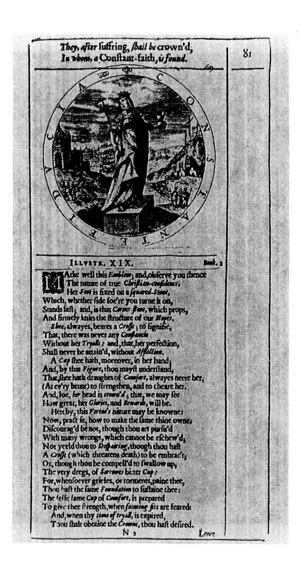

PLATE 6 *Constante fiducia*, from Wither's *A Collection of Emblemes* (1635),
emblem no. 81 Reproduced by courtesy of Glasgow University
Library, Department of Special Collections.

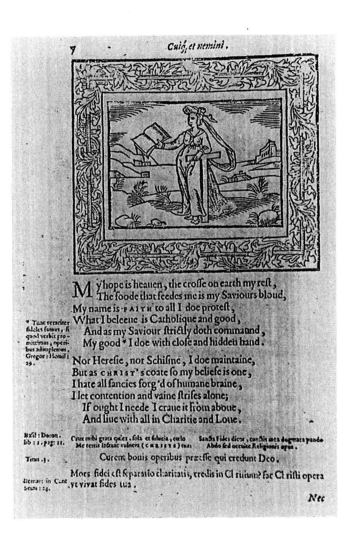

PLATE 7 *Cuique et nemini*, from Henry Peacham's *Minerva Britanna* (1612), emblem no. 7. Reproduced by courtesy of Glasgow University Library, Department of Special Collections.

PLATE 8 "A headless woman," from Thomas Combe's *The Theater of Fine Devices* (1614), emblem no. 16. The Huntington Library. Reproduced by permission of The Huntington Library, San Marino, California.

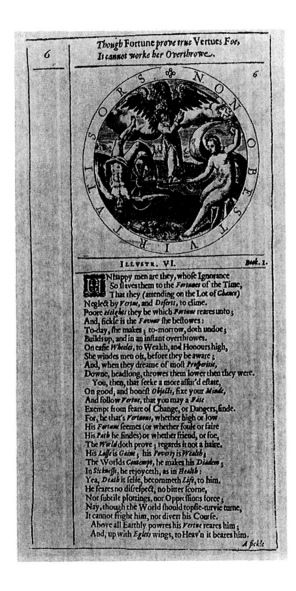

PLATE 9 *Non obest virtvti sors*, from Wither's *A Collection of Emblemes* (1635), emblem no. 6. Reproduced by courtesy of Glasgow University Library, Department of Special Collections.

PLATE 10 Giovanni Rost. *The Vindication of Innocence* (ca. 1549)
Italian tapestry. Galleria degli Uffizi, Florence. Reproduced by
courtesy of Galleria degli Uffizi, Florence.

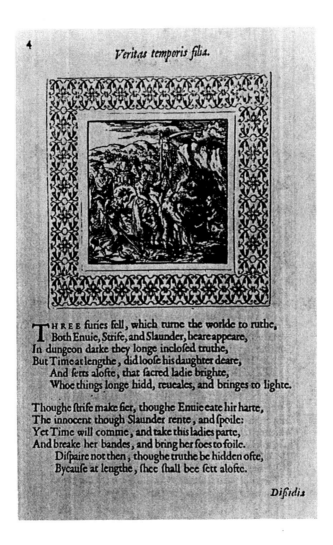

4

Veritas temporis filia.

THREE furies fell, which turne the worlde to ruthe,
  Both Enuie, Strife, and Slaunder, beare appeare,
In dungeon darke they longe inclofed truthe,
But Time at lengthe, did loofe his daughter deare,
  And fetts alofte, that facred ladie brighte,
  Whoe things longe hidd, reueales, and bringes to lighte.

Thoughe ftrife make fier, thoughe Enuie eate hir harte,
The innocent though Slaunder rente, and fpoile:
Yet Time will comme, and take this ladies parte,
And breake her bandes, and bring her foes to foile.
  Difpaire not then, thoughe truthe be hidden ofte,
  Bycaufe at lengthe, fhee fhall bee fett alofte.

Difidia

PLATE 11. *Veritas filia temporis*, from Whitney's *A Choice of Emblemes* (Leyden, 1586), emblem no. 4. Reproduced by courtesy of Glasgow University Library, Department of Special Collections.

PLATE 12 Giovanni Rost. *Flora or Spring*. 16th century Italian tapestry.
    Galleria degli Uffizi, Florence. Reproduced by courtesy of
    Galleria degli Uffizi, Florence.

PLATE 13 Sandro Botticelli. *Primavera* (ca. 1476). Painting. Galleria degli Uffizi, Florence. Reproduced by courtesy of Galleria degli Uffizi, Florence.

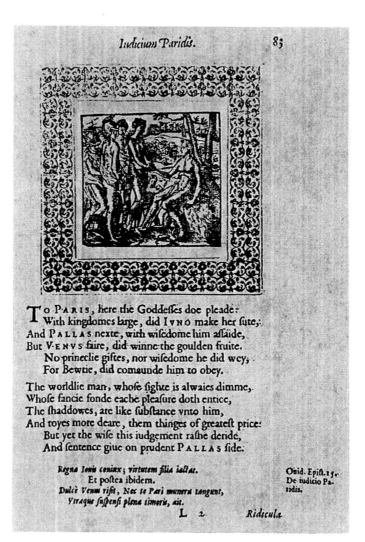

Iudicium Paridis.   83

To P A R I S, here the Goddesses doe pleade:
With kingdomes large, did I v n o make her sute,:
And P A L L A S nexte, with wisedome him assaide,
But V E N V S faire, did winne the goulden fruite.
   No princelie giftes, nor wisedome he did wey,
   For Bewtie, did comaunde him to obey.

The worldlie man, whose sighte is alwaies dimme,.
Whose fancie fonde eache pleasure doth entice,
The shaddowes, are like substance vnto him,
And toyes more deare, them thinges of greatest price:
   But yet the wife this iudgement rashe deride,
   And sentence giue on prudent P A L L A S fide.

Regna Iouis coniux; virtutem filia iactat.
   Et postea ibidem.
Dulcè Venm risit, Nec te Pari munera tangunt,
Ytraque suspensi plena timoris, ait.

Ouid. Epist.15.
De iudicio Pa-
ridis.

L 2.   *Ridicula*

PLATE 14 *Iudicium parides*, from Whitney's *A Choice of Emblemes* (Leyden, 1586), emblem no. 83. Reproduced by courtesy of Glasgow University Library, Department of Special Collections.

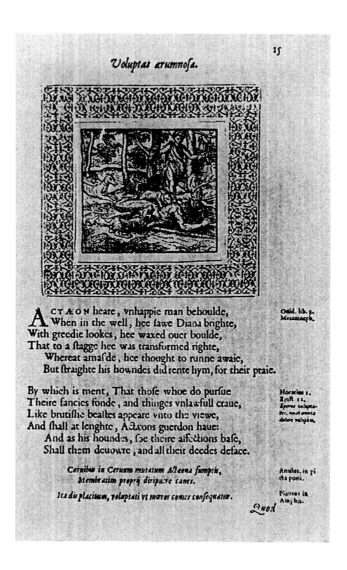

Voluptas ærumnosa.

15

ACTÆON heare, vnhappie man behoulde,
When in the well, hee sawe Diana brighte,
With greedie lookes, hee waxed ouer boulde,
That to a stagge hee was transformed righte,
   Whereat amasde, hee thought to runne awaie,
   But straighte his howndes did rente hym, for their praie.

Ovid. lib. 3. Metamorph.

By which is ment, That those whoe do pursue
Theire fancies fonde, and thinges vnlawfull craue,
Like brutishe bealtes appeare vnto the viewe,
And shall at lenghte, Actæons guerdon haue:
   And as his howndes, soe theire affections base,
   Shall them deuowre, and all their deedes deface.

*Horatius 1.
Epist. 1 1.
Spernit voluptat-
tes, nad emota
dolore voluptas.*

*Cornibus in Ceruum mutatum Acteona sumptis,
Membratim proprij diripuere canes.*

Ita dij placitum, voluptati vt mæror comes consequatur.

Quod

*Anulus, in pi
cta poesi.*

*Nascitur in
Amphib.*

PLATE 17 *Perseveranti dabitur*, from Wither's *A Collection of Emblemes* (1635), emblem no. 258. Reproduced by courtesy of Glasgow University Library, Department of Special Collections.

Index